United States Government Accountability Office

Report to Congressional Committees

I0426230

January 2012

BANK CAPITAL REQUIREMENTS

Potential Effects of New Changes on Foreign Holding Companies and U.S. Banks Abroad

GAO
Accountability * Integrity * Reliability

GAO-12-235

January 2012

BANK CAPITAL REQUIREMENTS

Potential Effects of New Changes on Foreign Holding Companies and U.S. Banks Abroad

G A O
Accountability * Integrity * Reliability

Highlights

Highlights of GAO-12-235, a report to congressional committees

Why GAO Did This Study

During the 2007-2009 financial crisis, many U.S. and international financial institutions lacked capital of sufficient quality and quantity to absorb substantial losses. In 2010, the Dodd-Frank Wall Street Reform and Consumer Protection Act (the Dodd-Frank Act) introduced new minimum capital requirements for bank and savings and loan (thrift) holding companies—including intermediate holding companies of foreign banks. Intermediate holding companies are the entities located between foreign parent banks and their U.S. subsidiary banks. These companies held about 9 percent of total U.S. bank holding companies' assets as of September 2011. The Dodd-Frank Act also required GAO to examine (1) regulation of foreign-owned intermediate holding companies in the United States, (2) potential effects of changes in U.S. capital requirements on foreign-owned intermediate holding companies, and (3) banks' views on the potential effects of changes in U.S. capital requirements on U.S. banks operating abroad. To conduct this work, GAO reviewed legal, regulatory, and academic documents; analyzed bank financial data; and interviewed regulatory and banking officials and market participants.

GAO makes no recommendations in this report. GAO provided a draft to the federal banking regulators (Federal Reserve, Federal Deposit Insurance Corporation and Office of the Comptroller of the Currency) for their review and comment. They provided technical comments that were incorporated, as appropriate.

View GAO-12-235. For more information, contact Thomas J. McCool at (202) 512-2642 or mccoolt@gao.gov.

What GAO Found

Foreign-owned intermediate holding companies can engage in the same activities as and generally are regulated similarly to their U.S. counterparts. The Board of Governors of the Federal Reserve System (Federal Reserve) oversees the regulation, supervision, and examination of foreign and U.S. bank and thrift holding companies. As of the end of 2010, four qualifying foreign-owned intermediate holding companies (exempt holding companies) were relying on a capital exemption, which allowed them to operate with significantly lower capital than U.S. peers. Federal Reserve officials noted that allowing capital to be held at the foreign parent bank (consolidated) level was consistent with its supervision for U.S. bank holding companies and met international standards for home-host supervision. The Dodd-Frank Act eliminated the capital exemption in order to enhance equal treatment of U.S.- and foreign-owned holding companies by requiring both types of companies to hold similar capital levels in the United States. As a result, these exempt holding companies must meet minimum capital standards that are not less than those applicable to Federal Deposit Insurance Corporation-insured depository institutions by July 2015.

The four exempt holding companies have been considering various actions to comply with new capital requirements, and the effects of eliminating the capital exemption on competition and credit cost and availability likely would be small. Specifically, these companies are considering raising capital, decreasing their holdings of risky assets, restructuring, or adopting a combination of these actions. GAO's analysis of loan markets suggests that the elimination of the capital exemption likely would have a limited effect on the price and quantity of credit available because the affected banks have relatively small shares of U.S. loan markets, which are competitive. These four companies accounted for about 3.1 percent of the loans on the balance sheets of all bank holding companies in the United States as of year end 2010. In addition, GAO's review of the academic literature and econometric analysis both suggest that changes in capital rules that affect the exempt companies would have a limited effect on loan volumes and the cost of credit and add minimally to the cumulative cost of new financial regulations. Although the impact on the price and quantity of credit available may vary across regions, modeling limitations restricted GAO's ability to identify regional differences.

Market participants expressed uncertainty about how changes in capital requirements might affect the competitiveness of U.S. banks operating abroad, partly because international regulatory capital requirements have yet to be implemented. The largest internationally active U.S. banks derived about one-third of their 2010 revenues from operations abroad. They face a variety of domestic and foreign competitors and are subject to multiple regulatory regimes. Bank officials expressed uncertainty about how changes in capital requirements will affect their cost of capital, lending ability, and competitiveness. Furthermore, they were concerned that fragmented or conflicting regulations across national jurisdictions might restrict banks' ability to use capital efficiently. Many U.S. banks GAO interviewed expressed concerns about the added costs of compliance with multiple regulatory regimes and the impact of the Act on the global competitiveness of U.S. banks, but these concerns would need to be considered against the potential benefits of a safer and sounder financial system.

_____ **United States Government Accountability Office**

Contents

Figures

Abbreviations

CCS	comprehensive consolidated supervision
CRD3	Capital Requirement Directive 3
CRD4	Capital Requirement Directive 4
DOJ	Department of Justice
DSGE	dynamic stochastic general equilibrium model
FBSEA	Foreign Bank Supervision Enhancement Act of 1991
FDIC	Federal Deposit Insurance Corporation
FTC	Federal Trade Commission
G-20	The Group of Twenty
GDP	gross domestic product
HHI	Herfindahl-Hirschman Index
IBA	International Banking Act of 1978
OCC	Office of the Comptroller of the Currency
OTS	Office of Thrift Supervision
SEC	Securities and Exchange Commission
SIFI	systemically important financial institution
UK	United Kingdom
VAR	vector autoregression model

United States Government Accountability Office
Washington, DC 20548

January 17, 2012

The Honorable Tim Johnson
Chairman
The Honorable Richard C. Shelby
Ranking Member
Committee on Banking, Housing, and Urban Affairs
United States Senate

The Honorable Spencer Bachus
Chairman
The Honorable Barney Frank
Ranking Member
Committee on Financial Services
House of Representatives

The 2007-2009 financial crisis revealed that many U.S. and international financial institutions lacked capital of sufficient quality and quantity to absorb substantial losses.[1] In response, banking regulators around the world moved to strengthen requirements for capital adequacy. In the United States, the Dodd-Frank Wall Street Reform and Consumer Protection Act (Dodd-Frank Act) introduced new capital requirements for bank and savings and loan (thrift) holding companies.[2] These requirements also apply to intermediate holding companies of foreign banking organizations (hereafter, such foreign banking organizations will be referred to as foreign parent banks or foreign banks).[3] These intermediate holding companies held approximately $1.6 trillion in U.S. assets in 2011, representing about 9

---

[1] Capital is a source of long-term funding, contributed largely by an institution's equity stockholders and its own returns in the form of retained earnings, that provides institutions with a cushion to absorb unexpected losses.

[2] Pub. L. No 111-203, § 171, 124 Stat. 1376, 1435 (2010). This section is also known as the Collins Amendment. A bank or thrift holding company owns or controls one or more banks or thrifts or owns or controls one or more bank or thrift holding companies. The company at the top of the ownership chain is commonly called the top-tier entity.

[3] Foreign banks may have their U.S. subsidiaries owned or controlled by an intermediate holding company in the United States (the organization between the subsidiary bank and the foreign parent bank) primarily to take advantage of tax or regulatory benefits.

percent of total U.S. bank holding companies' assets.[4] The Dodd-Frank Act requires these holding companies to meet minimum risk-based capital and leverage requirements that are not less than those applicable to depository institutions that the Federal Deposit Insurance Corporation (FDIC) insures. These requirements are intended to improve the capital and liquidity positions of such holding companies so that they may survive periods of financial and economic stress—thereby making the financial system more stable and reducing the likelihood or severity of future financial crises.

Section 174(b) of the Dodd-Frank Act requires us to study the effects of the new U.S. capital requirements on foreign-owned intermediate holding companies, taking into account the principles of national treatment and equality of competitive opportunity, which accord foreign banks the opportunity to compete in the United States on the same basis as domestic banks. This report examines (1) the regulation of foreign-owned intermediate holding companies in the United States, (2) the potential effects of changes in U.S. capital requirements on foreign-owned intermediate holding companies, and (3) banks' views on the potential effects of changes in U.S. capital requirements on U.S.-owned banks operating abroad.

To describe how foreign bank and thrift holding companies are regulated in the United States, we reviewed laws and regulations relevant to federal and state bank and thrift holding companies, regulatory documentation, and published reports, testimonies, speeches and articles; interviewed a state bank regulator, the European Commission (a European Union entity that, among other things, sets out general capital rules that each of the 27 European Union member countries can adopt at their discretion), bank holding companies, and industry experts; and reviewed prior GAO reports. In addition, we received written responses to questions from the European Banking Authority (European banking regulator) and attended a foreign bank conference on the implications of new capital rules. To assess the potential effects of changes in capital requirements for foreign-owned intermediate holding companies, we reviewed section 171 of the Dodd-Frank Act and proposed and final capital rules for foreign-owned intermediate holding companies and related comment letters. We also reviewed various proposed and final international capital rules. In addition, we reviewed Securities and Exchange Commission (SEC)

---

[4]Data as of September 30, 2011 according to the Board of Governors of the Federal Reserve System (Federal Reserve).

regulatory filings of foreign bank holding companies. Moreover, we interviewed officials from the European Commission, foreign and U.S. bank holding companies, credit rating agencies and industry experts on the effects of the new capital requirements on foreign banks operating in the United States. We used the Herfindahl-Hirschman Index (HHI)—a measure of industry concentration that reflects both the number of firms in the industry and each firm's market share—to track loan market concentration.[5] We compared market shares for foreign-owned intermediate holding companies (that were and were not subject to U.S. capital requirements) and U.S. bank holding companies. We obtained data on assets of foreign-owned intermediate holding companies and U.S. bank holding companies from SNL Financial—a private financial database. We obtained a list of foreign-owned intermediate holding companies and information on whether they were subject to U.S. capital requirements from the Board of Governors of the Federal Reserve System (Federal Reserve), which is the consolidated regulator for all bank and thrift holding companies in the United States.[6] We also obtained the views of foreign and domestic banks, credit rating agencies, and industry experts on the cost of capital and lending.

To estimate the effect of capital requirements on the cost and availability of credit we developed a modified version of a model commonly used in the macroeconomics and monetary literature. The data for the model were obtained from Thomson-Reuters Datastream, the Federal Reserve, and the

---

[5]The HHI is one of the concentration measures federal agencies, including the Department of Justice (DOJ) and the Federal Trade Commission (FTC), use when assessing market concentration to enforce U.S. antitrust laws.

[6]The Dodd-Frank Act eliminated the Office of Thrift Supervision (OTS), which chartered federal savings and loan associations (thrifts) and savings and loan holding companies (thrift holding companies), and supervised federally and state-chartered thrifts and thrift holding companies. 12 U.S.C § 5413. Rulemaking authority previously vested in OTS was transferred to the Office of the Comptroller of the Currency (OCC) for federally chartered thrifts and to the Federal Reserve for thrift holding companies and their subsidiaries, other than depository institutions. 12 U.S.C. § 5412(b). Supervision of state-chartered thrifts was transferred to the FDIC. 12 U.S.C. § 5412(b)(2)(C). The transfer of these powers was completed on July 21, 2011, and OTS was officially abolished 90 days later (October 19, 2011). 12 U.S.C. §§ 5411, 5413. OTS supervised one foreign-owned intermediate thrift holding company, ING Direct Bancorp, which agreed in June 2011 to sell its U.S. banking operations (ING Direct USA) to Capital One Financial Corporation. This report does not discuss OTS's past oversight of thrift holding companies. The Federal Reserve noted that, to the extent possible, it will apply bank holding company supervision, capital requirements, and regulatory reporting requirements to thrift holding companies.

Federal Reserve Bank of St. Louis. Because of the limitations associated with the modeling technique and uncertainty in the parameter estimates, we compared our results with those of a wider body of research on the effects of bank capital on lending activity. We obtained and analyzed relevant empirical studies and applied the estimates from these studies to the expected changes in capital stemming from the elimination of the Federal Reserve's capital exemption for certain institutions.

To identify banks' views on the potential risks from changes in capital requirements on U.S. banks operating abroad, we interviewed officials from three U.S. bank holding companies that engaged in significant international operations and officials from the European Commission. We summarized studies and congressional testimonies of the potential effects on U.S. banks' funding costs, product pricing, and lending activity abroad.

For all of our research objectives, we obtained the views of officials from the Federal Reserve, Office of the Comptroller of the Currency (OCC), Office of Thrift Supervision (OTS), FDIC, and the U.S. Department of the Treasury. We also conducted assessments of the reliability of data obtained from SNL Financial and other sources and determined that they were reliable for our purposes. For additional information on the scope and methodology for this engagement, see appendix I.

We conducted this performance audit from December 2010 to January 2012 in accordance with generally accepted government auditing standards. Those standards require that we plan and perform the audit to obtain sufficient, appropriate evidence to provide a reasonable basis for our findings and conclusions based on our audit objectives. We believe that the evidence obtained provides a reasonable basis for our findings and conclusions based on our audit objectives.

Background

Foreign banks have been cited as important providers of capital to the U.S. economy. According to Federal Reserve data, as of September 30, 2011, 216 foreign banks from 58 countries had banking operations in the United States. They held about $3.4 trillion, or about 22 percent of total U.S. banking assets; about 25.7 percent of total U.S. commercial and industrial loans; about 17.5 percent of total U.S. deposits; and about 14.9 percent of total U.S. loans.

Organization of Foreign Banks in the United States

Foreign banks may operate in the United States under several different structures, which include branches, agencies, subsidiary banks, representative offices, Edge Act corporations, Agreement corporations, and commercial lending companies (see table 1). Most operate through branches and agencies because as extensions of the foreign parent bank, they do not have to be separately capitalized and can conduct a wide range of banking operations.

Table 1: U.S. Operations of Foreign Banks, as of September 30, 2011

Dollars in billions

Organizational structure	Number of entities	Total assets	Description
Branches and agencies	246	$2,207	Branches and agencies may be licensed under federal or state law. They are not separate legal entities from their foreign parents. Federal branches have limited authority to take deposits, but may generally conduct the activities that a national bank can conduct. Agencies have more restricted deposit-taking authority but may undertake a broad range of banking activities. They generally are not FDIC-insured, and are not subject to U.S. capital requirements.[a]
Subsidiary banks	50	1,031	Subsidiary banks are chartered in the United States with shares owned or controlled by a parent foreign bank. They are separate legal entities from their foreign parents. They have the same banking powers and legal or regulatory restrictions as those of any other domestic bank. As such, they are subject to U.S. capital requirements.
Representative offices	138	Not applicable	Representative offices allow foreign banks to attract business for the parent bank and to develop correspondent relationships with local U.S. banks. However, they cannot engage in banking activities, although they may conduct administrative functions such as receiving checks to forward to their home offices and handling the signing of loan papers.
Edge Act/ Agreement corporations	9	7.5	Edge Act corporations are established as separate legal entities and may conduct a range of international banking and other financial activities in the United States. By agreement with the Federal Reserve, state-chartered Agreement corporations essentially have the same powers as Edge Act corporations.
Other entities	18	109.7	Other entities include commercial lending companies/investment companies and savings associations. For example, commercial lending companies are specialized nondepository institutions authorized under state law. They may engage in borrowing and lending activities and have numerous other powers. They may maintain credit balances but may not accept deposits.
Total	**461**	**$3,355**	

Sources: GAO and Federal Reserve data.

[a]Before December 1991, a limited number of foreign branches had obtained FDIC deposit insurance under provisions of the International Banking Act of 1978 and thus were allowed to accept retail deposits (currently up to $250,000 per depositor). But passage of the Foreign Bank Supervision Enhancement Act of 1991 prohibits any foreign branch from applying for federal deposit insurance. Foreign branches that had received insured deposits were grandfathered (allowed to continue to receive insured retail deposits). As of June 30, 2011, 10 such foreign branches operate. A foreign bank that wishes to accept insured deposits may do so through a de novo subsidiary or acquiring a separately chartered U.S. bank or thrift subsidiary.

Both domestic banks and U.S. subsidiary banks of foreign banks may be owned or controlled by a bank holding company. Holding companies are legally separate entities from their subsidiary banks, are subject to separate capital requirements, and are supervised and regulated by the

Federal Reserve. In the United States, bank holding companies are common and function as the top-tier entity in the corporate structure. In many foreign countries, notably in Europe, the deposit-taking bank is the top-tier entity in the corporate structure and bank holding companies are less common. According to the Federal Reserve, as of September 30, 2011, there were 29 foreign-owned intermediate holding companies in the United States. This report focuses on changes to the capital requirements for these entities under the Dodd-Frank Act.

Bank and thrift organizations are required to hold capital so that certain parties, such as depositors and taxpayers, would not be harmed if the bank or thrift faced unexpected substantial losses. There are many forms of capital, the strongest of which do not have to be repaid to investors, do not require periodic dividend payments, and are among the last claims to be paid in the event of bankruptcy. Common equity, which meets all of these qualifications, is considered the strongest form of capital. Weaker forms of capital have some but not all of the features of common equity. National banking regulators classify capital as either tier 1—currently the highest-quality form of capital and includes common equity—or tier 2, which is weaker in absorbing losses.[7] Different entities within a banking organization may have different capital requirements. For example, a subsidiary bank and a broker-dealer in the same corporate structure may be required to hold different levels of capital, and those capital requirements are established and supervised by different regulators.

International Efforts to Enhance Bank Supervision and Stability of the Financial System

In the 1980s, U.S. and international regulators recognized that common borrowers and complex products and funding sources had made the world's financial markets increasingly interconnected. Regulators also acknowledged that bank regulatory capital standards generally were not sensitive to the risks inherent in a bank's activities and that distressed or failing large, internationally active banks posed a significant global risk to the financial system. These concerns underscored the need for international regulatory coordination and harmonization of capital standards. As a result, in 1988 the Basel Committee on Banking Supervision (Basel Committee) adopted a risk-based capital

---

[7]Tier 1, or core, capital consists primarily of common equity. Tier 2 is supplementary capital and includes limited amounts of subordinated debt, loan loss reserves, and certain other instruments.

framework known as the Basel Capital Accord (Basel I).[8] Basel I aimed to measure capital adequacy (that is, whether a bank's capital is sufficient to support its activities) and establish minimum capital standards for internationally active banks. It consisted of three basic elements: (1) a target minimum total risk-based capital ratio of 8 percent and tier 1 risk-based capital ratio of 4 percent, (2) a definition of capital instruments to constitute the numerator of the capital-to-risk weighted assets ratio, and (3) a system of risk weights for calculating the denominator of the ratio. While the framework was designed to help improve the soundness and stability of the international banking system, reduce some competitive inequalities among countries, and allow national discretion in implementing the standards, it did not explicitly address all types of risks that banks faced. Rather, it addressed credit risk, which the Basel Committee viewed as the major risk banks faced at the time.[9] Over time it became apparent to bank regulators that Basel I was not providing a sufficiently accurate measure of capital adequacy because of the lack of risk sensitivity in its credit risk weightings, financial market innovations such as securitization and credit derivatives, and advancements in banks' risk measurement and risk management techniques. The accord was revised and enhanced multiple times after 1988 because of its shortcomings. For example, in 1996, Basel I was amended to take explicit account of market risk in trading accounts.[10] The market risk amendment allowed banks to use internal models of risks to determine regulatory capital levels. Table 2 identifies some key features of capital regime enhancements to the Basel accords.

---

[8]The framework is outlined in the July 1988 International Convergence of Capital Measurement and Capital Standards. Established in 1974, the Basel Committee seeks to improve the quality of banking supervision worldwide in part by developing broad supervisory standards. Its members represent central bank and regulatory officials from Argentina, Australia, Belgium, Brazil, Canada, China, France, Germany, Hong Kong, India, Indonesia, Italy, Japan, Korea, Luxembourg, Mexico, the Netherlands, Russia, Saudi Arabia, Singapore, South Africa, Spain, Sweden, Switzerland, Turkey, the United Kingdom, and the United States. The Basel Committee's supervisory standards are also often adopted by nonmember countries.

[9]Credit risk is the potential for loss resulting from the failure of a borrower or counterparty to perform on an obligation.

[10]Market risk is the potential for loss resulting from movements in market prices, including interest rates, commodity prices, stock prices, and foreign exchange rates. Generally, under the market risk amendment, a bank's internal models are used to estimate the 99th percentile of the bank's market risk loss distribution over a 10-business-day horizon (in other words, a solvency standard designed to exceed trading losses for 99 of 100 10-business-day intervals).

Table 2: Basel Capital Accord Framework, from 1988 through 2010

Capital regime	Year adopted by Basel Committee	Year(s) to be implemented	Risk enhancements	Minimum ratio of capital to risk-weighted assets	
Basel I	1988	1992	• Credit risk	Tier 1[a]	4%
				Total[b]	8%
Basel I market risk amendment	1996	1996	• Market risk		
Basel II	2004	2011	• Credit risk • Operational risk[c] • Market risk	Tier 1	4%
				Total	8%
Basel II.5 market risk amendment	2009	2011	• Market risk (updates 1996 market risk amendment)		
Basel III	2010	2013-2019	• Higher counterparty credit risk charges • New leverage ratio (on- and off-balance-sheet assets) • Improved quality and increase of capital • New liquidity ratios	Tier 1	6%
				Common equity tier 1[d]	4.5%
				Total	8%
				Additional capital requirements	
				Capital conservation buffer[e]	2.5%
				Countercyclical buffer[f]	0-2.5%
				Leverage ratio (a non-risk-based ratio)[g]	Currently set at 3%, with final percent to be determined

Sources: GAO analysis of Basel accords capital requirements and Barclays Capital.

[a]Tier 1 ratio is tier 1 capital divided by risk-weighted assets.

[b]The total risk-based capital ratio consists of the sum of tier 1 and tier 2 capital divided by risk-weighted assets. Tier 1 capital consists primarily of common equity. Tier 2 capital includes limited amounts of subordinated debt, loan loss reserves, and certain other instruments.

[c]Operational risk is the potential for unexpected financial losses due to a wide variety of institutional factors including inadequate information systems, operational problems, breaches in internal controls, and fraud.

[d]Common equity tier 1 ratio is common equity to risk-weighted assets.

[e]The capital conservation buffer, composed of common equity tier 1, is to be used by financial institutions to absorb losses during periods of financial and economic stress. The ratio is calculated as tier 1 capital minus regulatory deductions divided by total risk-weighted assets.

[f]The countercyclical buffer would be in effect during periods of excessive credit growth. The buffer would be set by each national authority with respect to the loan book and other credit exposures in its jurisdiction, and would be applied on a consolidated level on a weighted-average basis.

[g]The leverage ratio is tier 1 capital divided by average total assets (not adjusted for risk) plus certain off-balance-sheet exposures.

Basel II, adopted in June 2004, aims to better align minimum capital requirements with enhanced risk measurement techniques and encourage banks to develop a more disciplined approach to risk management.[11] It consists of three "pillars": (1) minimum capital requirements, (2) a supervisory review of an institution's internal assessment process and capital adequacy, and (3) effective use of disclosure to strengthen market discipline as a complement to supervisory efforts. Basel II established several approaches (of increasing complexity) to measuring credit and operational risks. The "advanced approaches" for credit risk and operational risk use parameters determined by a bank's internal systems as inputs into a formula supervisors developed for calculating minimum regulatory capital. In addition, banks with significant trading assets, which banks use to hedge risks or speculate on price changes in markets for themselves or their customers, must calculate capital for market risk using internal models.[12] The advanced approaches allow some bank holding companies to reduce capital from the levels required under Basel I. Large internationally active U.S. holding companies are implementing the first qualification phase—known as the parallel run—of the Basel II advanced approaches.[13] Although some of these large companies have begun to report Basel II capital ratios to their bank regulators, they still are subject to Basel I

---

[11]In June 2004, the Basel Committee published *Basel II: International Convergence of Capital Measurement and Capital Standards: A Revised Framework*.

[12]The advanced approaches generally apply to large internationally active banks. According to the U.S. Basel II advanced approaches rule, such banks are defined as those with consolidated total assets of $250 billion or more or with consolidated total on-balance-sheet foreign exposure of $10 billion or more.

[13]Prior to the Dodd-Frank Act, the four phases for the advanced approaches qualification were (1) the parallel run—four consecutive quarters in which a bank meets the qualification requirements and is subject to the Basel I rules but simultaneously calculates its risk-based capital ratios under the advanced approaches; (2) the first transitional period—a period of at least four consecutive quarters in which the bank computes its risk-based capital ratios using the Basel I rule and the advanced approaches rule, and required risk-based capital must be at least 95 percent of the Basel I requirement; (3) the second transitional period—a period of at least four consecutive quarters in which the bank computes its risk-based capital ratios using the Basel I rule and the advanced approaches rule, and required risk-based capital must be at least 90 percent of the Basel I requirement; and (4) the third transitional period—a period of at least four consecutive quarters in which the bank computes its risk-based capital ratios using the Basel I rule and the advanced approaches rule, and required risk-based capital must be at least 85 percent of the Basel I requirement. The Dodd-Frank Act had the effect of eliminating the transitional periods as they would apply in the United States and established a permanent capital floor.

capital requirements, as are other U.S. banks. Financial institutions in most other industrialized countries are subject to the Basel II capital standards. In response to the 2007-2009 financial crisis, Basel II was amended in 2009 by Basel II.5 to enhance the measurements of risks related to securitization and trading book exposures.[14]

Also in response to the 2007-2009 financial crisis, in 2010, the Basel Committee developed reforms, known as Basel III, which aim to improve the banking sector's ability to absorb shocks arising from financial and economic stress, whatever the source; improve risk management and governance; and strengthen banks' transparency and disclosures. The reforms target (1) bank-level, or microprudential, regulation to enhance the resilience of individual banking institutions to periods of stress and (2) systemwide risks that can build up across the banking sector as well as the amplification of these risks over time. These two approaches to supervision are complementary, as greater resilience at the individual bank level reduces the risk of systemwide shocks. Specifically, Basel III significantly changes the risk-based capital standards for banks and bank holding companies and introduces new leverage and liquidity requirements.[15] The new standards include a higher minimum common equity capital requirement of 4.5 percent of risk-weighted assets (the capital needed to be regarded as a viable concern); a new capital conservation buffer of 2.5 percent to provide a cushion during financial shocks to help companies remain above the 4.5 percent minimum; and more stringent risk-weights on certain types of risky assets, particularly securities and derivatives. Basel III also defines capital more narrowly than the previous accords. The new common equity tier 1 capital measure is limited mainly to common equity because common equity is generally the most loss-absorbing instrument during a crisis.

---

[14]Revisions to the Basel II market risk framework, July 2009 (updated December 31, 2010, February 2011), and Guidelines for computing capital for incremental risk in the trading book, July 2009.

[15]Basel III: A Global Regulatory Framework for More Resilient Bank and Banking Systems, December 2010.

U.S. Regulation of Foreign-Owned Holding Companies Intended to Achieve Equivalency with Domestic Counterparts

U.S regulation of foreign-owned intermediate holding companies is intended to be equivalent to regulation of domestic counterparts to help ensure that foreign bank operations have the opportunity to compete on a level playing field in the U.S. market. Several laws enacted since 1978 have shaped the regulation of foreign-owned intermediate holding companies and other foreign-owned banking operations. The International Banking Act of 1978 (IBA) is the primary federal statute regulating foreign bank operations in the United States.[16] In passing IBA, Congress adopted a policy of "national treatment," the goal of which is to allow foreign banks to operate in the United States without incurring either significant advantage or disadvantage compared with U.S. banks. To implement this policy, IBA brings branches and agencies of foreign banks located in the United States under federal banking laws and regulations. IBA and subsequent laws and regulations give foreign banks operating in the United States the same powers and subject them to the same restrictions and obligations as those governing U.S. banks, with some adaptations for structural and organizational differences.[17] For example, most foreign banks' operations are conducted through branches, and they generally can engage in the same activities as branches of U.S. banks. However, the U.S. branches of foreign banks are prohibited by law from acquiring deposit insurance from FDIC, and therefore may not accept retail deposits, whereas branches of U.S. banks can.[18]

In 1991, Congress passed the Foreign Bank Supervision Enhancement Act (FBSEA).[19] This Act, which amended IBA, authorizes the Federal Reserve to oversee all foreign bank operations in the United States.[20] Foreign banking organizations seeking to establish subsidiaries, branches, or agencies in the United States must apply for an operating

---

[16]Pub. L. No. 95-369, 92 Stat. 607 (1978).

[17]For example, foreign and U.S. banking institutions can engage in interstate branch banking and nonbanking activities such as securities underwriting and both are subject to reserve requirements, federal supervision, and capital adequacy standards.

[18]As previously noted in the report, a few foreign branches were exempted (grandfathered). Retail deposits are deposits of $250,000 or less.

[19]Pub. L. No. 102-242 tit. II subtit. A, 105 Stat. 2236, 2286 (1991).

[20]The Federal Reserve has regulatory authority for overseeing U.S. and foreign banks' international banking activities, which it administers through Regulation K. 12 C.F.R. § 211.20(a). It conducts supervisory activities through the 12 Federal Reserve Banks across the United States.

charter from either OCC (national charter or federal license) or state banking agency (state license). The Federal Reserve must also approve these applications. The Federal Reserve's approval process involves determining the soundness of the foreign parent bank's activities. Specifically, the Federal Reserve assesses, among other factors, the extent to which the home country supervisor (1) ensures that the foreign parent bank has adequate procedures for monitoring and controlling its activities globally, (2) obtains information on the condition of the foreign bank and its subsidiaries and offices outside the home country through regular reports of examination and audits, (3) obtains information on the dealings and relationships between the foreign bank and its affiliate companies, and (4) receives from the bank consolidated financial reports for analyzing the bank's global financial condition.

Another important requirement in the Federal Reserve's approval process includes assessing the quality of supervision provided by the applicant's home country supervisor. Specifically, the Federal Reserve determines the extent to which (1) the home country supervisor evaluates prudential standards, such as capital adequacy and risk asset exposure, on a global basis, and (2) the foreign parent bank is subject to comprehensive consolidated supervision—that is, the home country supervisor monitors the organization's overall operations across all legal subsidiaries and national jurisdictions. If the Federal Reserve is satisfied with the bank applicant's safety and soundness and the quality of the home country supervision, it can approve the foreign bank applicant (including its bank and nonbank affiliates) to do business in the United States. As the host country consolidated supervisor, the Federal Reserve retains full oversight authority over the foreign bank's U.S. operations.[21]

The Federal Reserve's determination that an institution is subject to comprehensive supervision or regulation on a consolidated supervision (CCS) basis by the appropriate authorities in its home country is an institution-specific finding.[22] If the Federal Reserve determined that a foreign bank was not subject to CCS, it still could approve the bank's

---

[21]U.S.-owned banks with foreign operations are generally regulated and supervised in the same manner. This meets elements of consolidated bank supervision and home-host supervisor relationship under the Basel Committee's "Core Principles Methodology."

[22]12 U.S.C. § 3105(d)(2)(A); see also item 15 of Attachment A to Federal Reserve Form FR K-2. International Applications and Prior Notifications under Subpart B of Regulation K.

GAO-12-235 Bank Capital Requirements

application if it found that the home country supervisor actively was working to establish arrangements for such supervision and all other factors were consistent with approval.[23]

FBSEA also established uniform standards for all U.S. operations of foreign banks, generally requiring them to meet financial, management, and operational standards equivalent to those required of U.S. banking organizations. For example, FBSEA required the Federal Reserve to establish guidelines for converting data on the capital of foreign banks to the equivalent risk-based capital measures for U.S. banks to help determine whether they meet the U.S. standards. Additionally, foreign banks' U.S. operations must be examined regularly for unsafe or unsound banking practices and are subject to regulatory financial reporting requirements similar to those for their U.S. counterparts.

The Gramm-Leach-Bliley Act permitted foreign and U.S. bank holding companies to become financial holding companies, which are authorized to engage in a wider range of financial activities (such as insurance underwriting and merchant banking) compared with bank holding companies.[24] In response to the Gramm-Leach-Bliley Act, the Federal Reserve modified its long-standing practice of applying its capital adequacy standards to foreign-owned intermediate holding companies. Specifically, in its January 5, 2001, Supervision and Regulation Letter 01-1, the Federal Reserve provided an exemption from complying with its capital adequacy guidelines (capital exemption) to foreign banks that are financial holding companies.[25] The Federal Reserve's supervisory letter stated that this action was consistent with its treatment of domestic banks and financial holding companies. Officials noted that domestic firms were expected to hold capital on a consolidated basis at the parent level, not

[23]The Federal Reserve also must consider whether the home country supervisor has adopted and implemented procedures, or is developing a legal regime or participating in multilateral effort to combat money laundering.

[24]Pub. L. No. 106-102, 113 Stat. 1338 (1999). The Gramm-Leach-Bliley Act allows those bank holding companies that meet certain capital, managerial, and other requirements to engage in securities underwriting, merchant banking, and insurance underwriting. As of September 30, 2011, 420 domestic bank holding companies and 40 foreign banking organizations had financial holding company status.

[25]Federal Reserve, *Application of the Board's Capital Adequacy Guidelines to Bank Holding Companies Owned by Foreign Banking Organizations* (Washington, D.C.: Jan. 5, 2001).

the intermediate holding company level. According to the supervisory letter, the capital exemption recognized that the foreign parent bank should be able to hold capital on a consolidated basis on behalf of its subsidiaries.

To qualify for the exemption, the foreign-owned intermediate holding company had to meet the standards for financial holding company status. Specifically, for a foreign bank to qualify as a financial holding company, the Federal Reserve was required to determine that the intermediate holding company's parent foreign bank was well capitalized and well managed on a consolidated basis.[26] Also, its U.S. depository subsidiaries were required to be well capitalized and well managed.[27] The bank subsidiaries of foreign bank organizations still were subject to the capital adequacy framework (risk-based capital and leverage standards) for insured depository institutions.[28]

A relatively small number of foreign-owned intermediate holding companies have relied on the capital exemption. The Federal Reserve reported that 6 of the approximately 50 foreign-owned intermediate holding companies used the capital exemption (exempt holding company) at some point during the period from 2001 to 2010. At the time the Dodd-Frank Act was enacted, in July 2010, 5 foreign-owned intermediate holding companies were relying on the capital exemption. By the end of December 2010, 1 of these 5 holding companies restructured its U.S. operations and no longer relied on the capital exemption. Exempt holding companies generally have operated with less capital than their foreign and domestic peers in the United States, with 1 such institution operating with negative risk-based capital ratios.

---

[26]The foreign parent bank must be well capitalized according to the capital standards in effect in the United States for bank holding companies. Currently, to be well capitalized, a bank holding company must meet a tier 1 risked-based capital ratio of 6 percent or greater, a total risked-based capital of 10 percent or greater, and certain other standards. See 12 CFR § 225.2(r). A bank holding company is considered well managed if the composite rating for its U.S. combined operations is at least satisfactory, and it has at least a satisfactory rating for management if such a rating is given. See 12 CFR § 22.5.2(s).

[27]If the foreign parent bank owns a U.S. depository bank subsidiary, the bank subsidiary must maintain a total risk-based capital ratio of at least 10 percent, a tier 1 risk-based capital ratio of at least 6 percent, and leverage ratio of at least 5 percent.

[28]See Federal Deposit Insurance Act, § 38, 64 Stat. 873 (1950) (codified, as amended, at 12 U.S.C. § 1831o).

U.S. Regulatory Reform Eliminated Capital Exemption for Certain Intermediate Holding Companies

The Dodd-Frank Act eliminated the capital exemption that the Federal Reserve provided to certain foreign-owned intermediate holding companies. The act requires that after a 5-year phase-in period after enactment of the act, these companies must satisfy the capital requirements at the intermediate holding company level. The change requires capital in the United States to support the foreign bank's U.S. operations conducted through a holding company and provides ready capital access for depositor and creditor claims in case the subsidiary depository or holding company fails and needs to be liquidated.[29] According to FDIC, the elimination of the capital exemption also was intended to better ensure that the foreign-owned intermediate holding company served as a "source of strength" for the insured depository institution.[30] Furthermore, according to FDIC, subjecting previously exempted foreign-owned intermediate holding companies to capital standards would discourage excessive financial leveraging. FDIC and some market participants have noted that the elimination of the exemption enhances the equal treatment of U.S. and foreign-owned holding companies by requiring both types of companies to hold similar capital levels in the United States. Figure 1, compares the capital structure of U.S.- and foreign-owned holding companies.

[29]This is considered a form of ring fencing, which refers to the practice by which local authorities set aside or shield assets of a local subsidiary from the failed institution and insist that local creditors get paid first, before any funds are transferred to satisfy claims made against the failed parent.

[30]Section 616(d) of the Dodd Frank Act confirmed the Federal Reserve's authority to require a bank or thrift holding company to serve as a source of strength to any subsidiary depository institution.

Figure 1: Capital Relationships in Foreign and Domestic Intermediate Holding Companies, after the Dodd-Frank Act

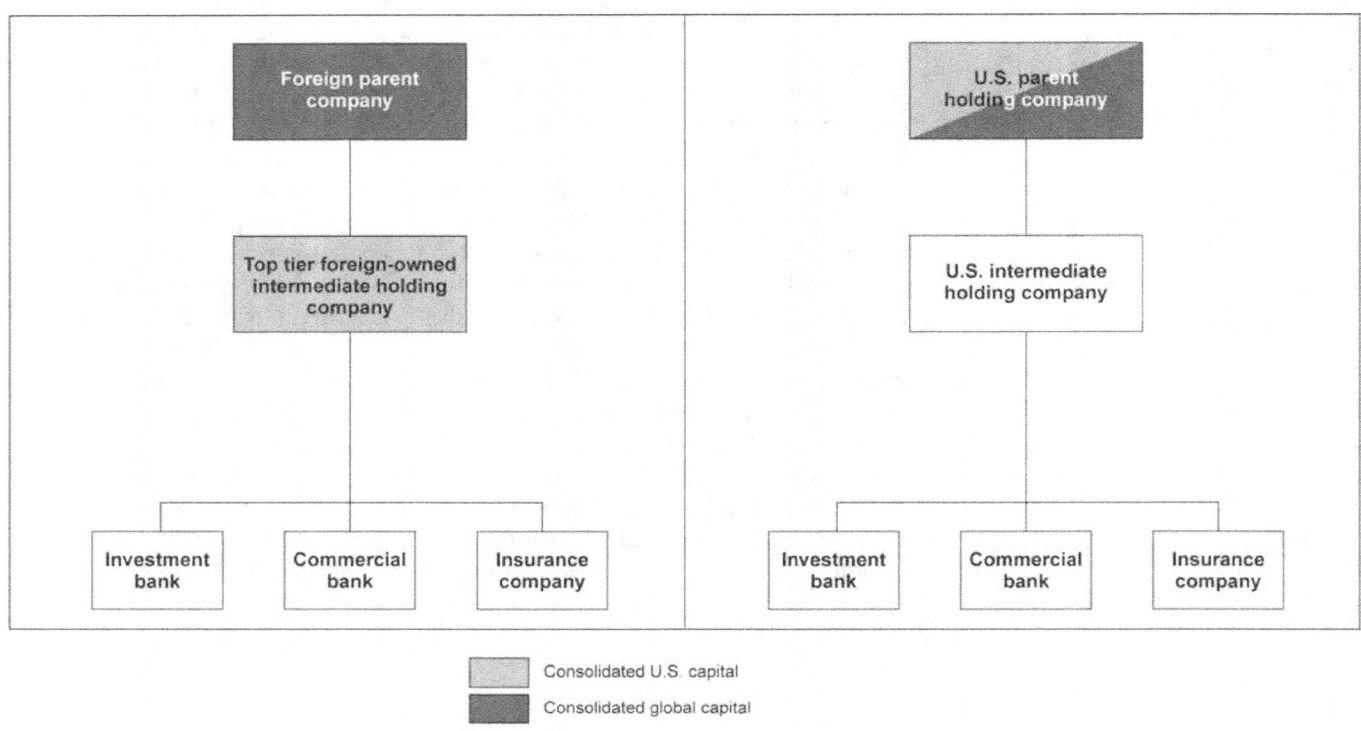

Consolidated U.S. capital

Consolidated global capital

Source: GAO.

Federal bank regulators have been finalizing proposed rules to implement the various capital requirements under the Dodd-Frank Act. According to regulators, they expect to issue final rules in 2012 but did not provide a specific date. The act requires that the previously exempted holding companies comply with the new capital adequacy guidelines by July 2015.[31] According to the Federal Reserve, it retains its supervisory authority to require any bank holding company to maintain higher levels of capital when necessary to ensure that its U.S. activities are operated in a safe and sound manner. This authority may be exercised as part of ongoing bank supervision or through the bank application process. We

---

[31]Capital requirements affecting hybrid instruments issued after the cutoff date of May 19, 2010, would be immediately applicable.

describe the different ways in which the exempted companies can satisfy the new capital requirements later in this report.

Stricter Capital Adequacy Standards Also Will Apply to Foreign and U.S. Holding Companies

In addition to eliminating the capital exemption for certain foreign-owned intermediate holding companies, the Dodd-Frank Act requires that bank and thrift holding companies—domestic or foreign—meet minimum risk-based capital and leverage requirements that are not less than those that apply to insured depository institutions. The existing minimum capital requirements (general risk-based capital guidelines) for insured depository institutions are largely based on Basel I (see fig. 1). Certain institutions—the largest internationally active holding companies and insured depository institutions—are subject to the U.S. implementation of the advanced approaches in the Basel II framework (advanced approaches capital guidelines). These large internationally active institutions are required to use their internal models to determine their risk-based capital levels, but under the Dodd-Frank Act they generally cannot hold less capital than would be required under the general risk-based capital guidelines for insured depository institutions.[32] These institutions will be required to calculate their capital under both the general risk-based capital guidelines and the advanced approaches capital guidelines.

The Dodd-Frank Act requires the federal banking regulators to implement the act's new requirements by January 2012. On June 14, 2011, the Federal Reserve, FDIC, and OCC approved an interagency final rule to implement the risk-based capital floors on the Basel II advanced approaches and published the final rule on June 28, 2011, thereby partially completing the requirements of the Dodd Frank Act.[33] However, the Federal Reserve has not addressed other items required under section 171, such as the phase-out of hybrid capital instruments from the

---

[32]Sections 171(b)(1) and (2) of the Dodd-Frank Act specify that the minimum leverage and risk-based capital requirements established under that section shall not be less than the "generally applicable" capital requirements, which shall serve as a floor for any capital requirements the agencies may require. Moreover, sections 171(b)(1) and (2) specify that the federal banking agencies may not establish leverage or risk-based capital requirements for covered institutions that are quantitatively lower than the generally applicable leverage or risk-based capital requirements in effect for insured depository institutions as of the date of enactment of the Dodd-Frank Act. 12 U.S.C. § 5371(b)(1)-(2).

[33]Risk-Based Capital Standards: Advanced Capital Adequacy Framework—Basel II; Establishment of a Risk-Based Capital Floor, 76 Fed. Reg. 37, 620 (June 28, 2011).

tier 1 capital of bank holding companies. It is expected that the Federal Reserve will address such items in 2012.

Finally, the Dodd-Frank Act also made changes that restricted the types of capital instruments that can be included in tier 1. Prior to the Act, the general risk-based capital guidelines for bank holding companies allowed such institutions to include hybrid debt and equity instruments in tier 1 capital whereas such instruments did not count in the tier 1 capital of insured depository institutions. Insured depository institution regulators (Federal Reserve, FDIC, and OCC) determined that such instruments did not have the ability to absorb losses as effectively as other forms of tier 1 capital. The specific requirements for the exclusion of hybrid debt or equity instruments from tier 1 capital vary according to the asset size and nature of the holding company.[34]

Overall Effects of Capital Changes for Exempt Foreign-owned Intermediate Holding Companies Likely to Be Limited

The elimination of the Federal Reserve's capital exemption for foreign-owned intermediate holding companies likely will result in exempt holding companies restructuring or taking other actions, but the overall effects of this change on competition among bank holding companies and cost and availability of credit are likely to be small for various reasons. First, our analysis of loan markets suggests that eliminating the exemption likely would have a limited effect on the price and quantity of credit available because the four banks most affected have relatively small shares of relatively competitive U.S. loan markets. Second, our review of the academic literature and our econometric analysis suggest that changes in capital rules that could affect certain foreign-owned intermediate holding companies would have a limited effect on loan volumes, and the increase in the cost of credit likely will add minimally to the cumulative cost of new financial regulations.

---

[34]Previously, the Federal Reserve allowed bank holding companies to use hybrid capital instruments, such as trust-preferred securities and cumulative-preferred securities, to compose up to 25 percent of their tier 1 capital amount. Internationally active banks were limited to a 15 percent of tier 1 capital threshold for hybrid instruments. For a greater discussion of hybrid capital instruments and the potential effects of the restriction on institutions' operations, see GAO, *Dodd-Frank Act: Hybrid Capital Instruments and Small Institution Access to Capital*, GAO-12-237 (Washington, D.C.: Jan. 18, 2012).

Foreign Parent Banks May Restructure or Take Other Actions to Comply with New Requirements

Foreign parent banks may take a variety of actions, including restructuring, to comply with the new requirements, although most are waiting for final rules on capital requirements and other Dodd-Frank Act–related provisions before making a decision. To date, banking and other financial regulators have not issued final rules implementing many of the Dodd-Frank Act requirements. Foreign bank officials we interviewed told us that they needed a better understanding of all the new regulatory provisions in the Dodd-Frank Act before deciding what action to take. Most of these bank officials told us they have been monitoring how regulators are implementing certain Dodd-Frank Act provisions, and the final rules likely will have a great effect on their decisions. These provisions include the designation and orderly liquidation of systemically important financial institutions (SIFI) and a prohibition on proprietary trading.[35] One foreign bank official told us that implementation of these provisions could have a major impact on her bank's U.S. operations.

Additionally, questions about how the new Basel III accord and other global capital rules will be implemented and how they will interact with U.S. banking regulations have added to foreign banks' uncertainty about planning for compliance with the Dodd-Frank Act. For example, in November 2011, the Basel Committee introduced a framework for designating global SIFIs.[36] Under the Basel framework, global SIFIs would be required to hold additional capital to absorb losses to account for the greater risks that they pose to the financial system. Foreign bank officials we interviewed stated that it is too early to tell how new global requirements will interact with U.S. requirements under the Dodd-Frank Act.

Despite the uncertainties about the specifics of the regulations, foreign banks have been considering a variety of actions to comply with the act, according to officials we contacted. Eliminating the capital exemption will have the most significant impact on the four foreign-owned intermediate

---

[35]The Financial Stability Oversight Council (established under the Dodd-Frank Act) can designate a nonbank financial company as a systemically important financial institution (SIFI). Such an entity would be supervised by the Federal Reserve and would be required to comply with enhanced supervision and prudential standards consistent with the Dodd-Frank Act. 12 U.S.C. § 5325.

[36]On November 4, 2011, the Financial Stability Board, which is responsible for coordinating and promoting the implementation of international financial standards (such as the Basel III accord), designated 29 financial institutions as global SIFIs. See http://www.financialstabilityboard.org/about/mandate.htm.

holding companies that relied on it.[37] These exempt holding companies and their foreign parent banks can comply in several ways. First, foreign parents could issue securities (debt or equity) and inject the capital as equity into the intermediate holding companies. Second, they could change the mix of risky assets they hold. For example, banks must hold more capital against certain assets in their portfolio that are considered higher-risk. The exempt holding companies could sell off these assets and acquire higher-quality or less-risky assets. Third, they could pass down profits or retain earnings from foreign parents to U.S. holding companies. Fourth, foreign parents could restructure their U.S. operations by removing any activities not considered banking activities from the exempt holding companies.[38] Finally, the foreign parent banks could close the exempt holding companies and leave the U.S. banking market.

One foreign parent bank restructured its exempt holding company by deregistering it in the fall of 2010. Prior to restructuring, the exempt holding company had a bank subsidiary, a broker-dealer subsidiary, and several other subsidiaries. The bank accounted for a small percentage of the exempt holding company's consolidated assets and revenues, but the holding company would be subject to the new capital requirement because it was supervised as a bank holding company by the Federal Reserve. After the restructuring, the small bank became a subsidiary of one bank holding company, while the broker-dealer and the other nonbank entities became subsidiaries of a different holding company that is not a bank holding company and therefore not subject to bank holding capital requirements. The foreign bank stated that restructuring would better align both foreign parent bank and U.S. bank holding company with new capital requirements.

How the four foreign parent banks with exempt holding companies choose to comply will vary. For example, officials from one exempt holding company told us that the foreign parent bank might inject several billions of dollars in common equity into the intermediate U.S. holding company. Officials from a second exempt holding company told us they

---

[37]We interviewed officials from three of the banks that did not rely on the exemption and they all said that they did not expect to take any immediate action, including raising additional capital, because their holding companies already met the new capital requirement under the Dodd-Frank Act.

[38]Examples of nonbank activities are financial management, mortgage and investment banking, insurance, and broker-dealer activities.

were considering a combination of actions, including recapitalizing its holding company by retaining earnings, reducing the risky assets against which it must hold capital, and potentially restructuring the holding company. Officials from another exempt holding company said that it would review business activities under the holding company to reduce risky assets that would require holding higher amounts of capital. Finally, the fourth exempt holding company stated in its annual report to SEC that the holding company might restructure, increase its capital, or both.

Eliminating the Exemption Likely Will Have Limited Effects on Overall Competition and Credit

Given the size of the market and the holding companies affected, elimination of the capital exemption for foreign-owned holding companies under the Dodd-Frank Act likely will have limited effects on the overall competitive environment and the cost and availability of credit to borrowers. Our analysis assesses the impact of the four exempt holding companies exiting the U.S. banking market or raising additional capital to meet regulatory standards.

The Number and Market Shares of Exempt Holding Companies Are Small

The number of exempt holding companies and their shares of most national loan markets are small. As of December 31, 2010, four exempt holding companies relied on the Federal Reserve's capital exemption. These exempt holding companies accounted for about 3.1 percent of the loans on the balance sheets of all bank holding companies in the United States (see table 3).[39] Therefore, any actions they may take to respond to the elimination of the capital exemption likely will have a small effect on the overall credit market.

---

[39]Our analysis generally covers bank holding companies with total consolidated assets of $500 million or more. Including smaller bank holding companies in the analysis would reduce the fraction of loans on the balance sheets of exempt holding companies.

Table 3: Bank Holding Company Loan Market Shares, as of December 31, 2010 By Percentage

Loan market	Bank holding company type		
	Exempt foreign-owned	Nonexempt foreign-owned	U.S.
Total net loans and leases	3.1%	6.6%	90.3%
Residential construction loans	3.0	5.2	91.9
Nonresidential construction, land development, and other land loans	2.2	6.8	91.0
Agricultural real estate loans	10.4	1.5	88.1
Home equity lines of credit	1.8	6.2	92.0
First-lien residential mortgages	1.9	8.1	90.0
Junior-lien residential mortgages	1.9	10.1	88.0
Multifamily residential property loans	1.8	5.2	92.9
Owner-occupied commercial real estate loans	3.6	4.9	91.5
Nonowner-occupied commercial real estate loans	3.8	5.7	90.5
Agricultural production loans	11.4	3.0	85.7
Commercial and industrial loans	3.9	7.0	89.1
Consumer loans	1.5	6.7	91.7
Lease financing receivables	4.5	4.0	91.4

Sources: GAO analysis of Federal Reserve and SNL Financial data.

Note: Bank holding companies include top-tier bank holding companies and are grouped by type. Calculations are for domestic offices of bank holding companies only. Exempt and nonexempt holding companies were identified by the Federal Reserve as of December 31, 2010. Market shares may not sum to 100 percent because of rounding.

Exempt holding companies accounted for varying amounts of different types of loans. In 2010, they accounted for less than 5 percent each of the construction and land loans, residential real estate loans, commercial real estate loans, commercial and industrial loans, consumer loans, and leases on the balance sheets of bank holding companies in the United States. However, they accounted for more than 10 percent each of agricultural real estate loans and agricultural production loans. Although exempt holding companies and their foreign parent banks can take a variety of approaches to comply with the new capital rules, the effects of those approaches on credit markets—overall or in specific segments—likely will be small because of the relatively small share of the market that exempt holding companies hold.

Foreign Banks' Exit from Credit Markets Would Have a Limited Effect on Competition and Cost and Availability of Credit

U.S. credit markets likely would remain unconcentrated even if exempt holding companies exited the market and sold their loans to other bank holding companies. To assess the impact of eliminating the Federal Reserve's capital exemption on competition among bank holding companies, we calculated the HHI, a key statistical indicator used to assess the market concentration and the potential for firms to exercise market power.[40] As figure 2 shows, the HHI for the overall loan market for 2010 is well below 1,500—the threshold for moderate concentration—as are the HHIs for the 13 specific loan markets we analyzed.[41] Because these loan markets appear to be unconcentrated, bank holding companies in these markets likely have little ability to exercise market power by raising prices, reducing the quantity of credit available, diminishing innovation, or otherwise harming customers as a result of diminished competitive constraints or incentives at least at the national level. As we discuss later, to the extent that markets are segmented by regions, or small businesses are limited in their ability to access credit, these results may not hold for all customers.

[40]The HHI is one of the market concentration measures that government agencies, including the Department of Justice (DOJ) and the Federal Trade Commission (FTC), use when assessing concentration to enforce U.S. antitrust laws. DOJ and FTC often calculate the HHI as the first step in providing insight into potentially anticompetitive conditions in an industry. However, the HHI is a function of firms' market shares, and market shares may not fully reflect the competitive significance of firms in the market. Thus, DOJ and FTC use the HHI in combination with other evidence of competitive effects when evaluating market concentration. The HHI reflects the number of firms in the market and each firm's market share, and it is calculated by summing the squares of the market shares of each firm in the market. For example, a market consisting of four firms with market shares of 30 percent, 30 percent, 20 percent, and 20 percent has an HHI of 2,600 (900 + 900 + 400 + 400 = 2,600). The HHI ranges from 10,000 (if there is a single firm in the market) to a number approaching 0 (in the case of a perfectly competitive market). DOJ and FTC guidelines as of August 19, 2010, suggest that an HHI between 0 and 1,500 indicates that a market is not concentrated, an HHI between 1,500 and 2,500 indicates that a market is moderately concentrated, and an HHI greater than 2,500 indicates that a market is highly concentrated, although other factors also play a role in determining market concentration.

[41]For this analysis, we defined the market as the collection of bank holding companies for which we could obtain balance sheet data from the Federal Reserve's Consolidated Financial Statements for Bank Holding Companies (FR Y-9C) through SNL Financial. This definition excludes other types of institutions that make loans, including bank holding companies with less than $500 million in assets (which are not required to file form FR Y-9C), savings and loans and finance companies that are not subsidiaries of a bank holding company. Credit unions are another source of loans, and capital markets are yet another source of funds for certain entities. Thus, the HHIs we calculate may either understate or overstate the amount of concentration in loan markets, depending on the number and market shares of other credit providers.

Figure 2: Herfindahl-Hirschman Index of Concentration in Loan Markets, as of December 31, 2010

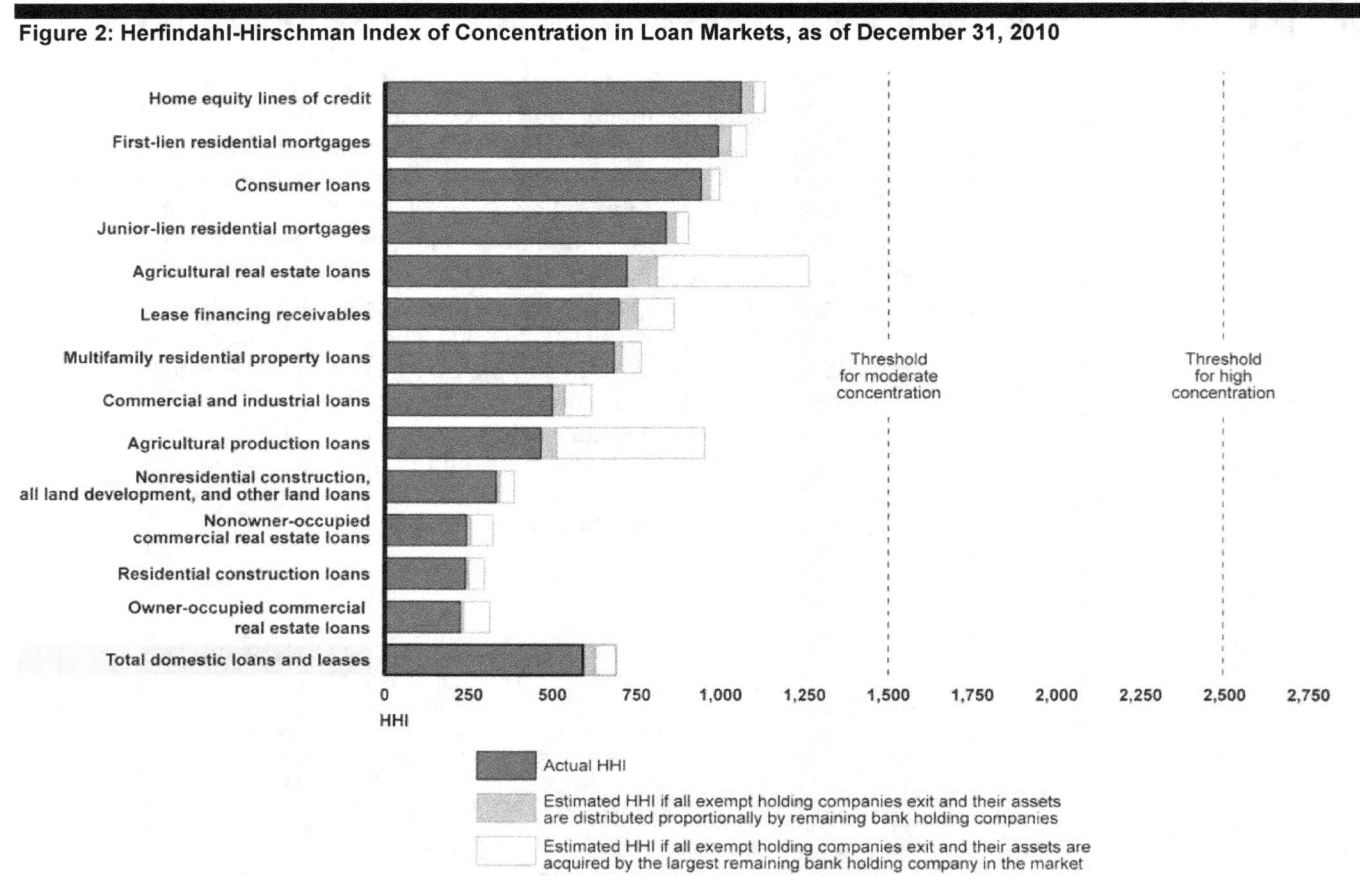

Threshold for moderate concentration

Threshold for high concentration

■ Actual HHI

▨ Estimated HHI if all exempt holding companies exit and their assets are distributed proportionally by remaining bank holding companies

☐ Estimated HHI if all exempt holding companies exit and their assets are acquired by the largest remaining bank holding company in the market

Source: GAO analysis of data from the Department of Justice, the Federal Reserve, the Federal Trade Commission, and SNL.

Faced with the elimination of the Federal Reserve's capital exemption and new minimum capital requirements under the Dodd-Frank Act, foreign banks with exempt holding companies could choose to divest their banks and exit the U.S. banking market. To estimate the effect of this particular response on loan market concentration, we estimated the change in loan market concentration on loan markets in two alternative scenarios in which all four of the exempt holding companies cease making loans and sell their portfolios to other bank holding companies. In the first scenario, the assets of exempt holding companies are acquired by remaining bank holding companies in proportion to their market share. In the second scenario, the assets of exempt holding companies are acquired by the largest bank holding company remaining in the loan market. Since not all exempt holding companies are likely to exit the U.S.

market, these scenarios provide estimates of the effect of the elimination of the Federal Reserve's capital exemption on market concentration in the most extreme cases.

Estimated changes in the HHIs for the overall loan market in these alternative scenarios indicate that the overall loan market is unlikely to become concentrated even if all exempt holding companies exited the U.S. market. As figure 2 shows, the overall loan market remains unconcentrated in both scenarios, suggesting that the remaining bank holding companies still would not have sufficient potential to use market power to increase loan prices above competitive levels or reduce the quantity of loans available to borrowers. Similar results were obtained when we applied the alternative scenarios to various segments of the credit market.

If Exempt Holding Companies Take Actions to Comply, Effects on the Cost and Availability of Credit Would Be Small

The total capital that the four exempt holding companies would need to raise to meet the same capital standards as their domestic counterparts is small relative to the total capital in the U.S. banking sector, thus limiting the effect on the cost and availability of credit. Of the four exempt holding companies remaining at the end of 2010, three have indicated they might undertake actions to comply with the minimum capital standards. As table 4 shows, to be considered as meeting the minimum capital requirements under the Dodd-Frank Act, the three exempt holding companies collectively would need $3.2 billion in additional capital, only $530 million of which would need to be in the form of tier 1 common equity to meet the leverage ratio requirement. This amount is less than 0.21 percent of the approximate $1.5 trillion in total equity outstanding for the U.S. banking sector. Two of the exempt holding companies have sufficient tier 1 capital and would be able to meet the total capital requirement by raising cheaper supplementary capital.[42] If the exempt holding companies decided to exceed the minimum requirements and meet the equivalent of the well-capitalized requirements for banks and thrifts, the difference, $6.6 billion, would be less than 0.44 percent of the total equity outstanding. Although this is a sizable capital deficit at the individual holding company level, it would represent a small shock to the aggregate U.S. banking sector.

---

[42]Supplementary capital is tier 2 capital.

Table 4: Capital Ratios and Capital Deficits for the Four Exempt Holding Companies Relative to Certain Capital Levels, as of December 31, 2010

	Tier 1 risk-based ratio	Total risk-based ratio (tier 1 + tier 2)	Tier 1 leverage ratio
Capital levels			
Dodd-Frank Act minimum capital requirements	4%	8%	3%-4%[a]
Well-capitalized standard[b]	6%	10%	5%
Exempt holding companies' capital ratios			
Company 1	Exceeds minimum	Does not meet minimum	Does not meet minimum
Company 2	Exceeds minimum	Does not meet minimum	Exceeds minimum
Company 3	Exceeds minimum	Does not meet minimum	Exceeds minimum
Company 4[c]	Does not meet minimum	Does not meet minimum	Does not meet minimum
Capital deficit (dollars in billions)			
Amount needed to meet Dodd-Frank Act minimum capital			
Company 1	0	$0.99	$0.53
Company 2	0	1.23	0
Company 3	0	0.97	0
Company 4[c]	$10.3	14.2	21.5
Total company 1–company 4	**$10.3**	**$17.4**	**$22.0**
Total company 1–company 3	**0**	**$3.19**	**$0.53**
Amount needed to be well capitalized[b]			
Company 1	0.7	$2.7	$3.76
Company 2	0.8	2.3	0.91
Company 3	0.5	1.6	0.68
Company 4[c]	12.2	16.2	31.6
Total company 1–company 4	**$14.2**	**$22.8**	**$37**
Total company 1–company 3	**$2.0**	**$6.6**	**$5.4**

Sources: GAO analysis of Federal Reserve and SNL Financial data.

[a]The minimum leverage ratio is 3 percent for bank and thrift holding companies with the highest examination ratings and not exhibiting rapid growth or other indicators of heightened risk, and for those that have implemented a risk-based capital measure for market risk, otherwise a 4 percent minimum leverage ratio applies.

[b]The analysis uses the explicit criteria for "well capitalized" that apply to banks and thrifts.

[c]Because of various factors, it is possble that company 4 will not take actions to meet the new requirements, and its foreign parent bank has been considering plans to restructure its operations, which would eliminate the need to raise capital. As a result, we include capital deficit totals that exclude company 4.

The remaining exempt holding company (company 4, in table 4) would be significantly below the new minimum capital requirements, with a capital shortfall of over $21.5 billion. However, domestic loans make up 11 percent of its total assets, while its broker-dealer operations are much larger. Therefore, maintaining a holding company designation, which creates a significant capital requirement on its entire asset pool, appears unlikely. As discussed earlier, the company has stated that it has been considering a variety of options, including restructuring. A restructuring may reduce the consolidated capital requirements applied to the foreign holding company and thus mitigate the need to raise capital to meet the new minimum capital requirements.[43]

However, as mentioned previously, exempt holding companies have other ways of adjusting to the elimination of the capital exemption and the forthcoming, more stringent capital requirements. For example, in addition to reducing assets or shifting portfolios toward less-risky assets, foreign parent banks also can issue new common equity (diluting existing shareholders), reduce or suspend dividend payments, or employ other strategies to increase retained earnings.[44] Because these alternatives each could imply different effects on credit markets, estimating the potential impact of heightened capital requirements for exempt holding companies on credit markets empirically would be useful (based on estimates of the relationship between capital and lending activity observed through rigorous analysis of data). We used a methodology designed to (1) leverage information about key relationships embedded in aggregated historical data, (2) account for feedback between economic variables, (3) control for other forces that might affect loan credit markets outside of capital positions, and (4) provide the opportunity to evaluate the dynamic response of loan volume growth and other important

---

[43]For the remainder of this section, we assume, based on information available to us and the degree of undercapitalization, that the fourth exempt holding company would restructure its operations.

[44]See appendix II for further discussion of the effects of reducing assets on the availability of credit.

variables to shocks to bank capital.[45] The methodology does not assume any particular manner of adjustment by the holding companies but focuses on the ultimate impact on loan volumes and spreads.

Although the econometric model we developed indicates that stronger capital requirements negatively affect lending activity, the impacts at the aggregate level are small. We evaluated the impact of the new requirements using two scenarios—exempt holding companies experienced a capital deficit when compared with the (1) minimum capital requirements under the Dodd-Frank Act or (2) the well-capitalized standard that applies to banks and thrifts. Specifically, our model suggests the elimination of the capital exemption would lead aggregate loan volumes to decline by roughly 0.2 percent even if the affected exempt holding companies desired to meet the equivalent of the well-capitalized standard (see table 5). If the affected banks desired to meet the minimum capital requirements under the Dodd-Frank Act, loan volumes would decline by less than 0.1 percent. Because the exempt holding companies would face capital deficits, the impact on the affected banks could be significant and would vary with the degree of undercapitalization. For example, loan growth would decline by 5.0 percentage points at company 1, 6.6 percentage points at company 2, and 7.9 percentage points at company 3 if the targeted total capital ratio was 10 percent under the well-capitalized standard, and total loan volumes would fall by $14.2 billion, or 0.2 percent of total loans for the banking sector. If the affected banks' targeted total capital ratio was 8 percent (that is, the minimum capital requirement), our model suggests total loan growth at the three banks would decline by $6.8 billion, or 0.09 percent of total loans for the banking sector.[46] However, these estimates

---

[45]Specifically, we employ the vector autoregression (VAR) methodology. See C. Lown and D. Morgan. "The Credit Cycle and the Business Cycle: New Findings Using the Loan Officer Opinion Survey," *Journal of Money, Credit, and Banking* 38, 6 (2006): 1575–97; and J. Berrospide and R. Edge (2010) 'The Effects of Bank Capital on Lending: What Do We Know, and What Does It Mean?'', International Journal of Central Banking, vol. 6 (December), 5-54. Our model is a version of the VAR models found in the macroeconomic and monetary literature extended to include a banking sector. It comprises four variables that capture supply, demand, output, and prices that make up the "macroeconomy." We then extend the model to include the credit market using various proxies for loan volumes, bank capital, loan spreads, and information on lending standards. See appendix I for a fuller discussion of the methodology, assumptions, and model.

[46]In our model, values reflect peak estimates reached from three to five quarters out, diminish after about 2 years, and assume no transition period.

may overstate the impact on aggregate loan volumes because we assume no transition period for adjusting to the higher capital requirements and that other banks do not immediately replace the decline in loan volumes at the affected institutions.[47]

Table 5: Aggregate Impacts of Eliminating the Capital Exemption

	Impact if the exempt holding companies needed to take actions to meet certain capital levels	
	Minimum capital requirement under the Dodd-Frank Act	Well capitalized standard[a]
Loan volumes		
GAO model	-0.09%	-0.19%
Estimate using other studies (average)	-0.06%	-0.12%
Lending spreads (basis points)		
GAO model	0.51	1.06
Estimate using other studies (average)	0.49	1.00

Sources: GAO and various empirical studies evaluating the relationship between bank capital and lending activity.

Notes: A basis point is a common measure used in quoting yield on bills, notes, and bonds and represents 1/100 of a percent of yield. Lending spreads are the commercial and industrial loan rate relative to the federal funds rate.

[a]The analysis uses the explicit criteria for "well-capitalized" that apply to banks and thrifts.

Because the capital exemption affects only a few institutions operating in highly competitive loan markets, the impact on the cost of credit, although uncertain, is likely to be small. Our model suggests that a capital shock equivalent to that implied by the elimination of the capital exemption (small at the aggregate level) would lead to an industrywide increase in lending spreads of a little over 1 basis point (0.01 percentage points).[48] If the exempt companies were measured against the minimum capital requirements, the impact on lending spreads would be less than 1 basis point. However, because the elimination would not result in a general

---

[47]We also elected to use commercial loans as the appropriate proxy for loan volumes in our model. The literature has found these loans to be more sensitive to capital. Using total loans for commercial banks and savings institutions produced effects that were less than half as large.

[48]Lending spreads measure loan rates relative to the banks' costs of funds. In our model, the lending spread is the difference between the commercial and industrial loan and federal funds rates.

shock across all banks, whether any impact on lending rates would be felt at the aggregate level is unclear. The competitive nature of loan markets makes passing on the higher cost of holding more capital to borrowers in the form of higher loan rates difficult for a bank experiencing a firm-specific capital shock. Because the loan markets are not highly concentrated and are competitive (as discussed earlier), the affected exempt holding companies likely would lose business to other banks if they chose to increase loan rates significantly.[49] Some studies have found evidence of a relationship between higher capital holdings and market share during and following banking crises.[50] To avoid losing business to well-capitalized institutions, the affected holding companies likely would reduce the amount of risky assets to some extent or undertake other actions rather than attempting to pass the full cost of holding additional capital to select customers. Appendix II contains more information on our analysis of these types of scenarios.

In general, our results for loan volumes and cost and availability of credit should be interpreted with caution because of the methodological and other limitations associated with our approach. For example, our estimates have wide confidence intervals suggesting considerable uncertainty in the results (see app. I for limitations). As such, considering our results in the context of a wider body of empirical literature is useful. Table 5 also includes the average impact on loan volumes and lending rates based on other studies combined with our calculation of the capital deficit stemming from the elimination of the capital exemption.[51] The results from our model, although larger for both loan growth and lending spreads, are consistent with the average we calculated from a number of empirical studies examining the relationship between bank capital and

---

[49]The higher loan rate may not be a social cost because it may reduce excessive lending. For example, see A. R. Admati, P. M. DeMarzo, M. F. Hellwig, and P. Pfleiderer, "Fallacies, Irrelevant Facts, and Myths in the Discussion of Capital Regulation: Why Bank Equity is *Not* Expensive," working paper, Stanford University Graduate School of Business (2010).

[50]See for example Allen Berger, and Christa Bouwman, "Bank Capital, Survival, and Performance around Financial Crises," Wharton Financial Institutions Center Working Paper 09-24 (2009).

[51]Each study allowed us to determine the impact of a 1 percentage point change in capital on loan volumes and lending rates. For example, in our model, a 1 percentage point change in capital translates to a change in loan volumes of about 2.41 percentage points. We then scale the estimates by the size of the expected capital deficit as a result of the elimination of the capital exemption.

lending activity. These studies represent a variety of methodologies, each with its own limitations. Nevertheless, even the largest estimate we identified in the literature still would imply a relatively small impact of the exemption on credit markets.

Particular segments of the market may be affected more than others. For example, customers in agricultural real estate and agricultural production loan markets may experience impacts larger than those suggested by the aggregate analysis. Similarly, two of the exempt holding companies have a significant presence in the western states, while another has a significant presence on the East Coast. While the impact on the price and quantity of credit available may vary across regions, modeling limitations restrict our ability to estimate potential regional differences. Such regional impacts should be mitigated to a significant extent by the national nature of many loan markets. This analysis becomes much more complicated and uncertain once consideration is given to the impact of the various provisions of the Dodd-Frank Act and Basel III, which may result in a large number of institutions looking to replace and raise capital if banks seek to exceed the new regulatory minimums by the same margin they exceed them now. However, our results indicate that the elimination of the capital exemption would add minimally, if at all, to the cumulative economic impacts of these regulations.

Market Participants Concerned about Differing Capital Regimes and Competitive Effects Abroad

Market participants expressed uncertainty about how changes in capital requirements might affect the competitiveness of U.S. banks operating abroad, partly because the international regulatory landscape remains unsettled. The largest internationally active U.S. banks derive a significant portion of their revenues from their operations abroad and are subject to multiple regulatory regimes. Regulatory capital requirements have become more stringent globally with the goal of reducing bank failures and creating a more stable financial system. However, bank officials we contacted were uncertain how changes in capital requirements might affect their competitiveness abroad and were monitoring U.S. and international reforms closely to assess any impact on their cost of capital, lending ability, and business competitiveness. They were concerned that fragmented or conflicting regulations might restrict banks' ability to use capital efficiently. Some U.S. banks believed that they might be at a competitive disadvantage to the extent that U.S. banks would be subject to higher capital requirements than banks from other countries. Finally, as major regulatory changes stemming from the Dodd-Frank Act, Basel III, and country-specific reforms are finalized and implemented, many U.S.

bank officials we interviewed expressed concerns about the added costs of compliance with multiple regulatory regimes.

The Largest Internationally Active U.S. Banks Derive Significant Revenues from International Operations

The largest internationally active U.S. banks maintained a strong presence in major foreign markets, where they derived close to one-third of their revenues on average in 2010 (see fig. 3). One of the largest internationally active U.S. banks derived close to 60 percent of its total revenues from foreign operations in 2010. In the last 3 years, revenues from foreign operations, although varying by bank and geographical region, have decreased slightly on a percentage basis.

Figure 3: Percentage and Dollars of Domestic versus Foreign Revenues of the Six Largest Internationally Active U.S. Banks, from 2005 to 2010

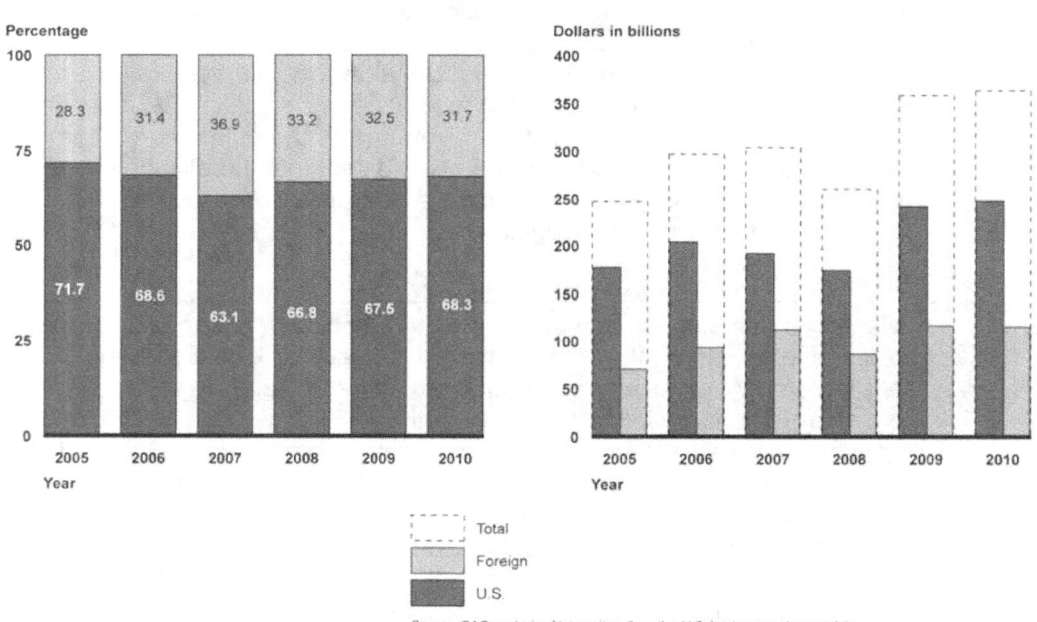

Source: GAO analysis of internationally active U.S. banks annual report data.

Generally, the largest internationally active U.S. banks divide their operations into the following four geographical regions: (1) North America; (2) Europe, the Middle East, and Africa; (3) Asia or Asia/Pacific; and (4) Latin America or Latin America/Caribbean.[52] As figure 4 shows, Europe, the Middle East, and Africa provided the biggest share (about 50 percent) of all foreign revenues. Revenues from the Asian and Pacific countries accounted for about 30 percent of foreign revenues compared with approximately 19 percent from Latin America.

Figure 4: Foreign Revenues of Six Largest Internationally Active U.S. Banks in 2010, by Region

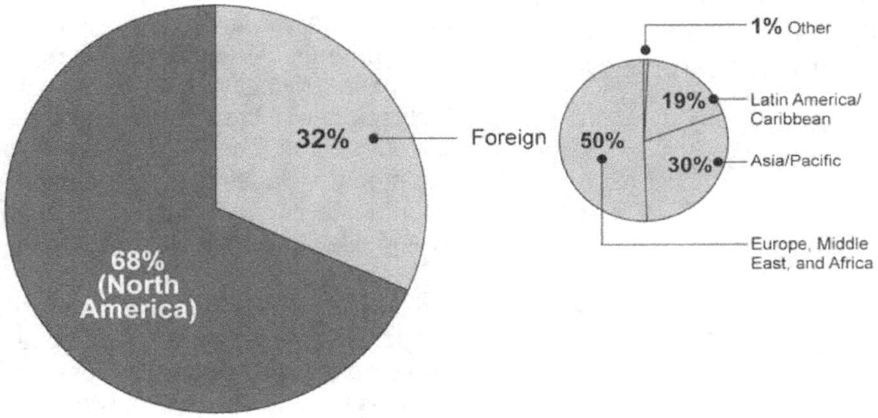

Source: GAO analysis of internationally active U.S. banks annual report data.

The large internationally active U.S. banks compete with large foreign-based banks and other internationally active U.S. banks across various product and geographic markets. Internationally active U.S. banks have varying lines of business. Although some focus on wholesale activities, one (Citigroup) is engaged in retail banking activities in more than 100 countries. In wholesale markets, some U.S. banks, like JPMorgan Chase and Bank of America, are active in making commercial and industrial

---

[52]In 2010, Bank of America, Citigroup Inc. and JPMorgan Chase & Co. reported revenues from foreign operations derived from Europe, the Middle East and Africa, Asia/Pacific, and Latin America. In addition, JPMorgan Chase & Co. and Bank of New York Mellon Corporation report foreign revenues that do not fit in any of the other segments in a category called "Other" (other non-U.S. revenues). The Goldman Sachs Group, Inc., and Morgan Stanley did not report revenues from Latin America, as their non-U.S. business activities are principally conducted through European and Asian locations.

GAO-12-235 Bank Capital Requirements

loans, while others, like Goldman Sachs and Morgan Stanley, hold a larger percentage of their assets as trading assets and engage in market making and trading in securities and derivative instruments. One of the largest internationally active U.S. banks, Bank of New York Mellon, primarily provides custody and asset management services and securities servicing. In this capacity, it competes with the largest U.S. banks and foreign-based banks that provide trust as well as banking and brokerage services to high-net-worth clients.

Internationally Active U.S. Banks Will Face Stricter Capital Regimes in Multiple Jurisdictions

In the wake of the 2007-2009 financial crisis, international jurisdictions have pursued more stringent capital requirements, and large, internationally active U.S. banks will be subject to the regulatory requirements of various foreign regulators. For example, in Europe, large internationally active U.S. banks will be subject to major new regulations, including those created by the Basel Committee and the European Commission.[53] The G-20 countries, which include the United States, adopted the Basel III agreements in November 2010, and the individual countries are responsible for incorporating the new agreements into national laws and regulations.[54]

On July 20, 2011, the European Commission published a legislative proposal known generally as Capital Requirement Directive 4 (CRD4) to implement the proposals of Basel III into European Union law. The commission staff we spoke with indicated that there are many legislative initiatives at the European Union level that could affect U.S. internationally active banks operating in Europe, but some key ones, in addition to CRD4, are the Capital Requirement Directive 3 (CRD3) and the Crisis Management Directive. CRD3 puts in place stricter capital

---

[53]The commission puts common European Union policies into practice, manages the European Union budget and programs, and can propose legislation to the European parliament.

[54]The Group of Twenty (or G-20) was established in 1999. Members originally consisted of representatives of 19 major economies and the European Union. The G-20 holds annual meetings at which finance ministers and central bank governors discuss measures to promote global financial stability and economic growth and development.

requirements, some of which became effective at the end of 2011.[55] Among other things, CRD3 requires banks to implement remuneration policies that are consistent with their long-term financial results and do not encourage excessive risk taking. For example, at least 40 percent of bonuses must be deferred 3-5 years and at least 50 percent must consist of equity or equity-like instruments or long-dated instruments that are convertible into tier 1 capital during emergency situations. The Crisis Management Directive will set out the different tools for resolutions of bank failures in Europe. It principally aims to provide the authorities with tools and powers to intervene in banks at a sufficiently early stage and is due to be adopted formally in November 2011.[56] This resolution authority also will apply to the European subsidiaries of U.S. banks.

In addition to the European Union regulatory initiatives, individual countries plan to implement additional measures. For example, the United Kingdom (UK) independently introduced a permanent levy on banks' balance sheets on January 1, 2011, to encourage banks to move to less-risky funding profiles, according to the UK's Her Majesty's Treasury. The levy applies to some UK banks, building societies, and UK operations of foreign banks with more than £20 billion in liabilities. The rate for 2011 will be 0.05 percent, and it will rise to 0.075 percent in 2012. In June 2010, France and Germany agreed to similar measures and have been enacting them.

| Differing International Regulations Could Affect U.S. Banks' Competitiveness Abroad | U.S. financial regulators and market participants have expressed concern about the extent to which the capital requirements and other financial regulations resulting from Basel III could be harmonized across national jurisdictions and how consistently they would be enforced. For example, U.S. regulators noted that the supervisory standard for how banks measure risk-weighted assets—the basis for regulatory capital ratios— |

---

[55]CRD3 implements the Basel Committee's July 2009 updates to the market risk framework, informally known as Basel II.5. The updates reflect strengthened standards for measuring market risk and holding capital against those risks, and improve transparency, especially for securitization activities. The United States is planning to implement Basel II.5 in 2012.

[56]In the event that problems arise with a bank in breach of the prudential requirements, a harmonized set of early intervention measures (such as clear powers to prohibit payment of dividends, impose additional reporting requirements, require the replacement of managers or directors, or require the cessation of certain risky activities) would be made available to supervisors.

under Basel III could be more transparent. In June 2011, the FDIC Chairman stated that European banks continued to in effect set their own capital requirements using banks' internal risk estimates—with risk-based capital determined by bank management assumptions, unconstrained by any objective hard limits and no leverage constraints.[57] Other, foreign regulators also stated that international differences in the calculation of risk-weighted assets could result from assigning inconsistent risk weights on the same types of assets and could undermine Basel III. Some foreign banks we interviewed told us that comparing risk-weighted assets across banks was challenging because of differing reporting, legal, and accounting frameworks. For example, comparisons of institutions from the United States with those from the European Union are difficult because U.S. banks still are transitioning from Basel I to Basel II and do not publicly report Basel II risk-based capital requirements. Conversely, banks in the European Union are operating under Basel II and are publicly reporting their risk-based capital ratios.

Additionally, U.S. regulators noted the potential for adverse competitive effects on banks with overseas operations from a Basel III provision for reciprocal countercyclical buffers.[58] If a regulator in one country issues an "excessive credit growth" declaration (that is, identifies a "bubble" when excess aggregate credit growth is judged to be associated with a buildup of systemwide risk), then all banks operating in that country would have to meet higher capital requirements. Regulators in other countries also could require banks operating in their countries to hold proportionately higher capital. For example, a U.S. bank operating in multiple countries would be subject to the cumulative effect of each country's additional requirements in times of excess aggregate credit growth, and U.S. banking regulators would have no say over these declarations.

[57]FDIC Chairman Sheila Bair, testimony before the Committee on Financial Services of the U.S. House of Representatives, June 16, 2011.

[58]The Basel Committee has expressed concern that the financial regulatory framework did not provide adequate incentives for firms to mitigate their procyclical use of leverage (debt). That is, firms tended to increase leverage in strong markets and decrease it when market conditions deteriorated, amplifying business cycle fluctuations and exacerbating financial instability. According to regulators, many financial institutions did not increase regulatory capital and other loss-absorbing buffers during the market upswing, when it would have been easier and less costly to do so. The Basel III countercyclical buffers are intended to help address concerns about procyclicality.

However, other factors may help ease concerns about inconsistent implementation of financial regulations. U.S. regulatory officials have observed that a high level of coordination among international regulators would help ensure that banks hold significantly more capital, that the capital will truly be able to absorb losses of a magnitude associated with the crisis without recourse to taxpayer support, and that the level and definition of capital will be uniform across borders. In addition, the quantity and quality of capital held by the largest internationally active U.S. and foreign banks has increased significantly in the past few years. Specifically, among the 50 largest global banks, tier 1 capital adequacy ratios have climbed from 8.1 percent in 2007 to 11.3 percent at the end of 2010. Since the end of 2008, the 19 largest bank holding companies in the United States that were subjected to stress tests increased common equity by more than $300 billion. Furthermore, European banks raised $121 billion in capital since Europe's June 2010 stress test exercise.

Conflicting Regulations Might Restrict Banks' Ability to Use Capital Efficiently

In addition to the specific concerns related to the implementation of Basel III, both U.S. and foreign bank officials we interviewed told us that they were concerned that fragmented or conflicting regulations in the United States and other jurisdictions might restrict banks' ability to use capital efficiently. According to U.S. and foreign bank officials, inconsistent capital requirements among multiple regulatory regimes may restrict banks' ability to move capital across jurisdictions. For example, according to regulators and U.S. banks we interviewed, since the 2007-2009 financial crisis, foreign regulators have become more sensitive to how much capital foreign entities in their jurisdiction hold. Some foreign bank regulators have required banks to "ring fence" capital on the balance sheet as a way to protect and hold dedicated capital for that bank subsidiary in their legal jurisdiction in case of financial difficulties or bankruptcy. Foreign bank regulators were concerned that the parent company would reallocate capital in their jurisdiction to fund the parent company located outside of their jurisdiction, potentially resulting in the subsidiary being undercapitalized. According to some banks we interviewed ring fencing would be costly for banks operating abroad as it restricts capital and requires systems for keeping operations segregated across countries.

In another example, U.S. bank officials noted that recent reforms have changed what types of capital instruments can be counted as tier 1 capital. As a result, U.S. banks may not have access to tax-efficient tier 1 instruments that foreign bank competitors can issue because of differences in national tax policies. Specifically, prior to the recent changes under the Dodd-Frank Act and Basel III, U.S. bank holding companies could issue tier 1 trust-preferred securities with dividend payments that were tax-deductible. With the exclusion of trust-preferred securities from tier 1, large internationally active banks likely will not have any tax-efficient alternative in the United States, while foreign banks in certain jurisdictions will continue to have access to certain capital instruments, such as noncumulative perpetual preferred shares, that confer some tax benefits because of local tax laws.[59]

Banks Could Face Additional Costs to Comply with Multiple Regulatory Regimes

As major regulatory changes stemming from the Dodd-Frank Act, Basel III, and country-specific reforms are finalized and implemented, many U.S. and foreign bank officials we interviewed expressed concerns about the added costs of compliance with multiple regulatory regimes. Because these regulations have not been implemented yet, how they may affect the operations of U.S. banks abroad is not known. For example, according to U.S. bank officials, they cannot yet estimate the cost associated with implementing and complying with the new risk-based capital and leverage requirements under Basel III. Moreover, implementation of key provisions of the Dodd-Frank Act and the new Basel III capital and liquidity requirements will be particularly challenging because of the number of related provisions that must be considered together. According to a testimony given by the Acting Comptroller of OCC, regulators have been trying to understand not only how individual provisions will affect the international competitiveness of U.S. firms, but also how the interactions of the various requirements of the Dodd-Frank Act and Basel III will affect U.S. firms domestically.[60]

According to testimony from an industry expert, areas other than the bank capital provisions of the Dodd-Frank Act can affect costs (including compliance costs and competition): prohibition of proprietary trading by banks, exclusion of the use of external credit ratings for determining risk weighting, regulations governing derivatives, the designation and regulation of SIFIs, and resolution of insolvent financial firms.[61] For

---

[59]See GAO-12-237.

[60]Acting Comptroller of the Currency John Walsh, testimony before the Committee on Financial Services of the U.S. House of Representatives, June 16, 2011.

[61]Hal S. Scott, Director of the Committee on Capital Markets Regulation; Professor and Director of the Program on International Financial Systems, Harvard Law School, testimony before the Committee on Financial Services of the U.S. House of Representatives, June 16, 2011.

GAO-12-235 Bank Capital Requirements

example, bank officials we interviewed told us that the Dodd-Frank Act's exclusion of the use of external credit ratings for determining risk weighting will create additional costs to U.S. banks. The banks would have to develop their own methods for performing these calculations, potentially putting them at a competitive disadvantage (including higher cost) internationally because European banks could still use such credit ratings, which are widely understood and used by investors. U.S. bank officials also noted that they would incur increased administrative costs under multiple regulatory regimes as they would have to implement and comply with multiple capital ratios, including those for the U.S. and foreign jurisdictions. Many U.S. banks GAO interviewed expressed concerns about the added costs of compliance with multiple regulatory regimes and the impact of the Dodd-Frank Act on the global competitiveness of U.S. banks, but these concerns would need to be considered against the potential benefits of a safer and sounder financial system.

Agency Comments

We provided a draft of this report to the FDIC, the Federal Reserve and OCC for their review and comment. Each of the federal banking regulators provided technical comments that were incorporated in the report, as appropriate.

We are sending copies of this report to appropriate congressional committees, FDIC, the Federal Reserve, OCC, and the Department of the Treasury, and other interested parties. In addition, the report is available at no charge on the GAO website at http://www.gao.gov.

If you or your staff have any questions about this report, please contact me at (202) 512-2642 or mccoolt@gao.gov. Contact points for our Offices of Congressional Relations and Public Affairs may be found on the last page of this report. GAO staff who made key contributions to this report are listed in appendix VI.

Thomas J. McCool
Director, Center for Economics
Applied Research and Methods

Appendix I: Objectives, Scope, and Methodology

The objectives of the report were to examine (1) the regulation of foreign-owned intermediate holding companies in the United States, (2) the potential effects of changes in U.S. capital requirements on foreign-owned intermediate holding companies, and (3) banks' views on the potential effects of changes in U.S. capital requirements on U.S.-owned banks operating abroad. This report focuses on intermediate holding companies owned by a foreign parent bank (that is, a foreign banking organization) and the largest internationally active U.S. banks based on their level of foreign business activity.[1] The foreign parent bank may have its U.S. subsidiaries owned or controlled by an intermediate bank or thrift holding company in the United States (the organization between the subsidiary bank and the foreign parent bank) primarily to take advantage of tax or regulatory benefits.[2] Under this corporate structure, the intermediate holding company represents the foreign parent bank's top-tiered legal entity in the United States and is regulated by the Board of Governors of the Federal Reserve System (Federal Reserve).

To describe how foreign holding companies are regulated and supervised in the United States, we reviewed relevant federal and state banking laws and regulations (such as the International Banking Act of 1978, Foreign Bank Supervision Enhancement Act of 1991, section 171 of the Dodd-Frank Wall Street Reform and Consumer Protection Act [Dodd-Frank Act], and New York state banking law). We reviewed regulatory documents such as the Federal Reserve's Consolidated Financial Statements for Bank Holding Companies—FR Y-9C.[3] Further, we reviewed supervisory guidance such as Supervision and Regulation Letter 01-1 (the capital exemption), the final rule that establishes a floor for the risk-based capital

---

[1] A foreign banking organization is defined as a company organized under the laws of a foreign country that engages in the business of banking.

[2] A bank or thrift holding company owns or controls one or more banks or thrifts, respectively, or one that owns or controls one or more bank or thrift holding company or owns or controls one or more bank or thrift companies. The company at the top of the ownership chain is commonly called the top-tier entity.

[3] The FR Y-9C is a Federal Reserve reporting form that collects basic financial data from a domestic bank holding company on a consolidated basis in the form of a balance sheet, an income statement, and detailed supporting schedules, including a schedule of off balance-sheet items. The information is used to assess and monitor the financial condition of bank holding company organizations, which may include parent, bank, and nonbank entities. The FR Y-9C is a primary analytical tool used to monitor financial institutions between on-site inspections and is filed quarterly as of the last calendar days of March, June, September, and December.

requirements applicable to the largest internationally active banks, relevant published reports, testimonies, speeches, articles, and relevant prior GAO reports.[4] We interviewed supervisory officials at the Federal Reserve, Federal Deposit Insurance Corporation (FDIC), Office of the Comptroller of the Currency (OCC), Office of Thrift Supervision (OTS), New York State Banking Department, and officials at the Department of the Treasury, the European Commission (a European Union entity that, among other things, through capital directives sets out general capital rules to be transferred into national law by each of the 27 European Union countries as they deem appropriate), foreign and U.S. bank holding companies, a foreign trade association, credit rating agencies, and law firms.[5] In addition, we received written responses to questions from the European Banking Authority (European banking regulator) and attended a conference on the implications of new capital rules for foreign banks.

To assess the potential effects of changes in capital requirements for foreign-owned intermediate holding companies, we reviewed section 171 of the Dodd-Frank Act, and proposed and final capital rules for foreign-owned intermediate holding companies and related comment letters. We reviewed various proposed and final international capital rules. We reviewed Securities and Exchange Commission (SEC) regulatory filings of foreign bank holding companies. We interviewed foreign bank regulators, foreign and U.S. bank holding companies, credit rating agencies, and industry experts on the effects of the new capital requirements on foreign banks operating in the United States. We also reviewed academic studies on the impact of higher capital requirements

---

[4]The Federal Reserve's Supervision and Regulation Letter 01-1 of January 5, 2001, permitted a foreign-owned intermediate holding company whose foreign parent bank qualified to become a financial holding company to be exempt from complying with capital adequacy standards. For the final rule on capital floors, see 76 Fed. Reg. 37.620 (June 28, 2011). According to the U.S. Basel II advanced approaches rule, internationally active banks are defined as those with at least $250 billion of consolidated total assets or at least $10 billion of consolidated total on-balance-sheet foreign exposure.

[5]The Dodd-Frank Act eliminated the OTS, which chartered federal savings and loan associations (thrifts) and savings and loan holding companies (thrift holding companies), and supervised federally and state-chartered thrifts and thrift holding companies. 12 U.S.C § 5413. Rulemaking authority previously vested in OTS was transferred to OCC for federally chartered thrifts and to the Federal Reserve for thrift holding companies and their subsidiaries, other than depository institutions. 12 U.S.C. § 5412(b). Supervision of state-chartered thrifts was transferred to FDIC. 12 U.S.C. § 5412(b)(2)(C). The transfer of these powers was completed on July 21, 2011, and OTS was officially abolished 90 days later (October 19, 2011). 12 U.S.C. §§ 5411, 5413.

on the cost of capital and lending and obtained the views of foreign and
domestic banks, credit rating agencies, and industry experts.

To assess the extent to which credit markets are likely to be affected by
removal of the capital exemption, we calculated market shares for each
group of bank holding companies in loan markets as of December 31,
2010. We obtained balance sheet data for bank holding companies as of
December 31, 2010, from SNL Financial, which reports data for bank
holding companies based on forms FR Y-9C submitted to the Federal
Reserve. In general, only top-tier bank holding companies with
consolidated assets of $500 million or more are required to submit FR Y-
9Cs. To avoid double-counting bank holding companies that are
subsidiaries of other bank holding companies, we obtained lists of
second-tier bank holding companies as of December 31, 2010, from the
Federal Reserve's National Information Center website and used this list
to drop any second-tier bank holding companies from our analysis.[6] Our
sample—our definition of the market—is thus the collection of top-tier
bank holding companies with consolidated assets of $500 million or more
that filed FR Y-9Cs with the Federal Reserve as of December 31, 2010.

We obtained lists of all top-tier foreign-owned intermediate holding
companies—both exempt and nonexempt—operating in the United States
as of December 31, 2010, from the Federal Reserve. We used these lists
to classify bank holding companies in our sample as one of three types:
exempt foreign-owned intermediate holding companies, nonexempt
foreign-owned intermediate holding companies, and U.S. bank holding
companies. We calculated the percentage of various types of loans on
the balance sheets of each group, including the following:

- total domestic loans and leases,

- residential construction loans,

- nonresidential construction loans and all land development and other
  land loans,

---

[6]The National Information Center is a central repository of data about banks and other
institutions for which the Federal Reserve has a supervisory, regulatory, or research
interest, including both domestic and foreign banking organizations operating in the United
States

- agricultural real estate loans,

- home equity lines of credit,

- first-lien residential mortgage loans,

- junior-lien residential mortgage loans,

- multifamily residential property loans,

- owner-occupied commercial real estate loans,

- nonowner-occupied commercial real estate loans,

- agricultural production loans,

- commercial and industrial loans,

- consumer loans, and

- leases.

We used amounts reported for domestic offices only so that our comparisons were consistent across foreign-owned intermediate holding companies and U.S. bank holding companies. A group's market share is the total dollar value of loans on the balance sheets of all bank holding companies in the group as a percentage of the total dollar value of loans on the balance sheets of all bank holding companies in the market.

To assess the extent to which the price of credit and the quantity of credit available are likely to be affected because of the removal of the capital exemption, we used the used the HHI to measure market concentration. The HHI is a key statistical indicator used to assess the market concentration and the potential for firms to exercise market power. The HHI reflects the number of firms in the market and each firm's market share, and it is calculated by summing the squares of the market shares of each firm in the market. For example, a market consisting of four firms with market shares of 30 percent, 30 percent, 20 percent, and 20 percent has an HHI of 2,600 (900 + 900 + 400 + 400 = 2,600). The HHI ranges from 10,000 (if there is a single firm in the market) to a number approaching 0 (in the case of a perfectly competitive market). That is, higher values of the HHI indicate a more concentrated market. Department of Justice and Federal Trade Commission guidelines as of

August 19, 2010, suggest that an HHI between 0 and 1,500 indicates that a market is not concentrated, an HHI between 1,500 and 2,500 indicates that a market is moderately concentrated, and an HHI greater than 2,500 indicates that a market is highly concentrated, although other factors also play a role in determining market concentration.[7]

We calculated the HHI for 2010 for each of the loan markets listed above. Each bank holding company is a separate firm in the market, and its market share is equal to the dollar value of loans on its balance sheet as a percentage of the total dollar value of loans on the balance sheets of all the bank holding companies in the market.

We also calculated the HHI for 2010 for each loan market in alternative scenarios in which exempt holding companies cease making loans and transfer the loans on their balance sheets to bank holding companies that remain in the market. In the first scenario, exempt foreign-owned intermediate holding companies' loans are distributed proportionally among remaining bank holding companies. In the second scenario, exempt foreign-owned intermediate holding companies' loans are acquired by the largest remaining bank holding company in the market.

A limitation of defining the market as the collection of top-tier bank holding companies that filed FR Y-9Cs with the Federal Reserve is that we exclude organizations that provide credit. For example, small bank holding companies—those with consolidated assets of less than $500 million—generally are not required to file form FR Y-9C. However, they do make loans. Other credit market participants include savings and loan holding companies, stand alone banks, savings and loan associations, credit unions, and finance companies not owned by bank holding companies. Capital markets are another source of funds for some borrowers. As a result, our estimates of market shares are likely overstated. Furthermore, our estimates of market concentration may be either understated or overstated, depending on the number and market shares of other credit providers.

---

[7]The HHI is one of the market concentration measures that government agencies, including the Department of Justice (DOJ) and the Federal Trade Commission (FTC), use when assessing concentration to enforce U.S. antitrust laws. DOJ and FTC often calculate the HHI as the first step in providing insight into potentially anticompetitive conditions in an industry. However, the HHI is a function of firms' market shares, and market shares may not fully reflect the competitive significance of firms in the market. Thus, DOJ and FTC use the HHI with other evidence of competitive effects when evaluating market concentration.

Another limitation of our analysis is that we implicitly assume that all loan markets are national in scope; that is, that credit provided by a bank holding company is available to any potential borrower, regardless of his or her respective geographic location. If loan markets are not national in scope, then our market share and market concentration estimates are unlikely to represent those that we would estimate for a specific subnational region, such as a state or metropolitan area. The market share and market concentration estimates for some regions likely would be greater than our national estimates, while others likely would be lower.

For this analysis, we relied on the Federal Reserve's FY-9C data that we obtained through SNL Financial and on information from the Federal Reserve on foreign banking organizations' top-tier intermediate holding companies in the United States. We conducted reliability assessment on these data by reviewing factors such as timeliness, accuracy, and completeness. We also conducted electronic testing to identify missing and out-of-range data. Where applicable, we contacted officials from the Federal Reserve to address questions about the reliability of the information. We found the data to be sufficiently reliable for our purposes.

To estimate the effect of capital ratios on the cost and availability of credit, we estimated a modified version of a vector autoregression (VAR) model commonly used in the macroeconomics and monetary literature. Our model closely follows Berrospide and Edge (2010) and Lown and Morgan (2006). The VAR consists of eight variables. The core variables that represent the macroeconomy are (1) real gross domestic product (GDP) growth, (2) GDP price inflation, (3) federal funds rate, and (4) commodity price index growth. As is pointed out in Lown and Morgan (2006), these four variables potentially make up a complete economy, with output, price, demand, and supply all represented. We capture the banking sector with four variables: (1) loan volume growth, (2) changes in lending spreads—commercial and industrial loan rates relative to a benchmark, (3) lending standards as measured by the net fraction of loan officers at commercial banks reporting a tightening of credit standards for commercial and industrial loans in the Federal Reserve's Senior Loan Officer Opinion Survey, and (4) the aggregate capital-to-assets ratio for the commercial bank sector. The addition of the latter four variables allows us to investigate the dynamic interaction between banks and the macroeconomy. The data were assembled from Thomson-Reuters Datastream and the Federal Reserve. We have relied on these data in our past reports and consider them to be reliable for our purposes here.

Using the estimated VAR system for the third quarter of 1990 to the
second quarter of 2010, we trace the dynamic responses of loan
volumes, lending spreads, and other macroeconomic variables to shocks
to the bank capital ratio. As a result, we can obtain quantitative estimates
of how bank "innovations" or "shocks" affect the cost and availability of
credit. Our base results rely on impulse response functions using the
following causal ordering of the variables: GDP, inflation, federal funds
rate, commodity spot prices, loan volumes, capital ratio, loan spreads,
and lending standards. However, our final estimates use the average of
the outcomes for the two different orderings of the variables: (1) where
the macro variables are given causal priority and (2) where the bank
variables are given causal priority. The VAR model, and the innovation
accounting framework, is laid out in greater detail in another GAO report.[8]

The VAR methodology, while containing some advantages over other
modeling techniques, has particular limitations, and therefore the results
should be interpreted with caution. First, the methodology potentially
overstates the quantitative effects of shocks on the economy and can be
difficult to interpret. Second, because the technique relies on past data, it
is subject to the criticism that past information may not be useful for
gauging future response due to policy changes. Third, to conduct
meaningful assessments of the impacts of shocks to the system, causal
priority is given to some variables over others. However, our results are
not particularly sensitive to this ordering, although we do obtain smaller
impacts of bank capital on lending activity with some alternative
orderings. To minimize this limitation, our estimates are an average of a
model where causal priority is given to the macroeconomic variables and
a model where causal priority is given to the bank variables. Last, in our
particular case the impulse response functions have wide confidence
intervals, suggesting considerable uncertainty in the results. Despite
these limitations, the VAR approach is considered to be a reasonable
alternative to other types of models. However, it is prudent to evaluate our
results in the context of the wider body of research on the effects of bank
capital on lending activity.

The studies we relied on for comparison are useful in that they represent
a variety of different modeling techniques ranging from VAR and cross-
sectional regression methodologies to more sophisticated dynamic

---

[8]See GAO-12-237.

stochastic general equilibrium (DSGE) modeling. None of these approaches are without limitations. For example DSGE models, although among the best for conducting counterfactual experiments and easy to interpret, are difficult to estimate and the techniques used to facilitate estimation can result in questionable results that are at odds with empirical observations. Nevertheless, by considering the body of evidence from different studies, we are able to provide some assessment of the reliability of our findings. However, the studies discussed in the report are included solely for research purposes and our reference to them does not imply we find them definitive.

To describe U.S. banks operating abroad and their services, major customers, and competitors, we used information obtained from interviews with some of the largest internationally active U.S. banks. We also analyzed audited financial statements in the annual reports for relevant companies. We selected the six largest internationally active U.S. banks based on their level of foreign business activity.[9] To identify banks' views on the potential risks from changes in capital requirements on U.S. banks operating abroad, we interviewed officials from the three U.S. bank holding companies that engaged in significant international operations. We also interviewed officials from the European Commission—a European Union entity that, among other things, through capital directives sets out general capital rules to be transferred into national law by each of the 27 European Union countries as they deem appropriate. We summarized relevant academic literature and regulatory studies and congressional testimonies on the potential effects on U.S. banks' funding costs, product pricing, and lending activity abroad. We also obtained the views of federal banking officials from the Federal Reserve, FDIC, OCC, and OTS, and officials from the Department of the Treasury.

We conducted this performance audit from December 2010 to January 2012 in accordance with generally accepted government auditing standards. Those standards require that we plan and perform the audit to obtain sufficient, appropriate evidence to provide a reasonable basis for our findings and conclusions based on our audit objectives. We believe that the evidence obtained provides a reasonable basis for our findings and conclusions based on our audit objectives.

---

[9]The bank holding companies are: Bank of America Corporation, The Bank of New Mellon Corporation, Citigroup Inc., The Goldman Sachs Group, Inc., JPMorgan Chase & Co., and Morgan Stanley.

Appendix II: Impact of Reducing the Risk-Weighted Assets of Exempt Holding Companies to Comply with New Requirements

Bank holding companies can take different approaches to comply with the new capital requirement in the Dodd-Frank Wall Street Reform and Consumer Protection Act. From 2001 to 2010, the Board of Governors of the Federal Reserve System granted capital requirement exemptions to six foreign-owned intermediate holding companies provided that the companies satisfied certain conditions, including having well-capitalized foreign parent banks.[1] As of the end of 2010, four foreign-owned intermediate holding companies continued to rely on a capital exemption from the Federal Reserve. The Dodd-Frank Act eliminated this exemption, and these exempt holding companies must now meet new capital requirements. Some of these exempt holding companies may choose to raise capital, while others may choose to deleverage by decreasing the risk-weighted assets on their balance sheets (or a combination thereof).[2] Although predicting the responses of the exempt holding companies to the higher U.S. bank capital requirements is a complex proposition, this appendix illustrates the potential effect on the availability of credit if the three exempt holding companies respond by reducing their balance sheets.[3]

If the exempt holding companies chose to reduce their balance sheets to meet new capital regulations, we estimate that the decrease would be small relative to the aggregate assets for the U.S. banking sector. As table 6 illustrates, the three exempt holding companies would need to decrease their risk-weighted assets by amounts ranging from $12.2 billion to as much as $15.3 billion to meet the minimum capital requirements

---

[1]Supervision and Regulation Letter 01-1 (January 5, 2001).

[2]Risk-weighted assets are the total assets and off-balance-sheet items held by an institution that are weighted for risks according to the federal banking agencies' regulatory capital standards.

[3]We excluded one exempt holding company from this analysis because of various factors. For example, the exempt holding company likely will restructure its U.S. operations. Officials from the bank did not respond to our request for a meeting to discuss potential actions.

Appendix II: Impact of Reducing the Risk-
Weighted Assets of Exempt Holding
Companies to Comply with New Requirements

under the Dodd-Frank Act.[4] While the scale of this deleveraging is large at the individual holding company level, it is small as a percentage of the total risk-weighted assets of the U.S. banking sector (see table 6). For example, although the exempt holding companies would have to reduce their balance sheets by 20 percent on average, the total decline in assets amounts to 0.44 percent of the $9.1 trillion in total risk-weighted assets for the aggregate U.S. banking sector. To meet the equivalent of the well-capitalized standards that apply to banks and thrifts, the exempt holding companies would need to reduce their risk-weighted assets by $65.8 billion, or roughly 0.7 percent of the total risk-weighted assets for the aggregate U.S. banking sector. This would require two of the exempt holding companies to decrease risk-weighted assets by roughly 38 percent and 34 percent, respectively.

Table 6: Decrease in Risk-Weighted Assets Necessary to Meet Certain Capital Levels

	Decline in risk-weighted assets to meet minimum capital requirements under the Dodd-Frank Act	Percentage of total U.S. banking sector assets	Decline in risk-weighted assets to meet well capitalized level	Percentage of total U.S. banking sector assets
Company 1	$12,313,113,000	0.13%	$26,516,093,000	0.29%
Company 2	$15,316,751,000	0.17	$23,175,154,000	0.25
Company 3	$12,176,820,000	0.13	$16,143,270,000	0.18
Total decline	**$39,806,684,500**	**0.44%**	**$65,834,517,000**	**0.72%**
Total risk-weighted assets for banking sector				**$9,141,452,000,000**

Sources: GAO analysis of Federal Reserve and SNL Financial data.

Note: The foreign parent of company 4 is considering plans to restructure its operations to eliminate the need to raise capital.

While the reduction in assets could entail the canceling of lines of credit and reduced lending by these institutions, our market share analysis detailed above suggests that other banks would service affected creditworthy borrowers at competitive rates. This shrinkage in risk-

---

[4]To meet the minimum capital requirements under the Dodd-Frank Act, a bank holding company would be required to maintain at a minimum a tier 1 risk-based capital ratio of 4 percent, a total risk-based capital ratio of 8 percent, and a leverage capital ratio of 4 percent, except that of a bank holding company that holds the highest supervisory rating is subject to a 3 percent minimum leverage ratio. The total risk-based capital ratio equals the sum of tier 1 and tier 2 capital divided by risk-weighted assets. Tier 2 capital includes limited amounts of subordinated debt, loan loss reserves, and certain other instruments. The tier 1 leverage capital ratio is tier 1 capital divided by average total assets.

Appendix II: Impact of Reducing the Risk-
Weighted Assets of Exempt Holding
Companies to Comply with New Requirements

weighted assets still could have implications for less-creditworthy borrowers, especially if a reduction in assets included lines of credit to customers who benefited from lower rates than they otherwise could receive at other institutions. However, rather than simply reducing the overall size of their portfolios, exempt holding companies also could shift the composition of their portfolios toward less-risky assets. For example, if the exempt holding companies were to sell assets with a 100 percent risk weighting and purchase an equivalent amount of assets with a 50 percent risk weighting, one would exceed the minimum capital requirements while the others would need to reduce their assets by an additional $1.2 billion and $1.8 billion. An adjustment of this type would imply a shift from commercial loans and commercial mortgages, which appear to be a significant portion of book of business for the three holding companies under consideration.

Appendix III: GAO Contact and Staff Acknowledgments

GAO Contact	Thomas J. McCool, (202) 512-2642 or mccoolt@gao.gov
Staff Acknowledgments	In addition to the contact listed above, Daniel Garcia-Diaz (Acting Director), Rachel DeMarcus, M'Baye Diagne, Lawrance Evans Jr., Colin Gray, Joe Hunter, Elizabeth Jimenez, Courtney LaFountain, Akiko Ohnuma, Marc Molino, Timothy Mooney, Patricia Moye, Michael Pahr, and Barbara Roesmann made key contributions to this report.

GAO's Mission	The Government Accountability Office, the audit, evaluation, and investigative arm of Congress, exists to support Congress in meeting its constitutional responsibilities and to help improve the performance and accountability of the federal government for the American people. GAO examines the use of public funds; evaluates federal programs and policies; and provides analyses, recommendations, and other assistance to help Congress make informed oversight, policy, and funding decisions. GAO's commitment to good government is reflected in its core values of accountability, integrity, and reliability.
Obtaining Copies of GAO Reports and Testimony	The fastest and easiest way to obtain copies of GAO documents at no cost is through GAO's website (www.gao.gov). Each weekday afternoon, GAO posts on its website newly released reports, testimony, and correspondence. To have GAO e-mail you a list of newly posted products, go to www.gao.gov and select "E-mail Updates."
Order by Phone	The price of each GAO publication reflects GAO's actual cost of production and distribution and depends on the number of pages in the publication and whether the publication is printed in color or black and white. Pricing and ordering information is posted on GAO's website, http://www.gao.gov/ordering.htm.
	Place orders by calling (202) 512-6000, toll free (866) 801-7077, or TDD (202) 512-2537.
	Orders may be paid for using American Express, Discover Card, MasterCard, Visa, check, or money order. Call for additional information.
Connect with GAO	Connect with GAO on Facebook, Flickr, Twitter, and YouTube. Subscribe to our RSS Feeds or E-mail Updates. Listen to our Podcasts. Visit GAO on the web at www.gao.gov.
To Report Fraud, Waste, and Abuse in Federal Programs	Contact: Website: www.gao.gov/fraudnet/fraudnet.htm E-mail: fraudnet@gao.gov Automated answering system: (800) 424-5454 or (202) 512-7470
Congressional Relations	Katherine Siggerud, Managing Director, siggerudk@gao.gov, (202) 512-4400 U.S. Government Accountability Office, 441 G Street NW, Room 7125 Washington, DC 20548
Public Affairs	Chuck Young, Managing Director, youngc1@gao.gov, (202) 512-4800 U.S. Government Accountability Office, 441 G Street NW, Room 7149 Washington, DC 20548

Please Print on Recycled Paper.